Microsoft™ BASIC

Second Edition

Microsoft™ BASIC

Second Edition

Ken Knecht

dilithium Press
Beaverton, Oregon

10   9   8   7   6   5   4   3   2   1

Library of Congress Cataloging in Publication Data

Knecht, Kenneth.
  Microsoft BASIC.
  Includes index.
  1. Basic (Computer program language)
I. Title.
QA76.73.B3K57   1982   001.64'24   82-14730
ISBN 0-88056-056-8

Microsoft™ is a registered trademark of Microsoft Corporation, Bellevue, Washington.

TRS-80™ is a registered trademark of the Radio Shack Division of Tandy Corporation, Fort Worth, Texas.

Printed in the United States of America

dilithium Press
P.O. Box 606
Beaverton, Oregon 97075

Table of Contents

Introduction

In the early 1970's, the computer hobby really sprang to life with the introduction of the Altair 8800 by MITS. The birth of this first 8-bit hobby computer was prompted by the introduction of Intel's 8080 microprocessor integrated circuit. By the way, when introduced, the 8080 microprocessor was said to cost $350.00. Now it can be purchased for about $6.95.

This early microcomputer ran the BASIC language. Who wrote this early version of BASIC? Why, Microsoft of course. The actual authors were Bill Gates and Paul Allen. With over one million installations, Microsoft Corporation continues to be a major supplier of BASIC interpreters for microcomputers.

This second edition of *Microsoft*™ *BASIC* describes the latest version of Microsoft BASIC: BASIC-80, release 5.0. While this release of BASIC-80 is the latest version of Microsoft BASIC, some popular microcomputers are supplied with a slightly different version. Fortunately, the differences are not great. If you understand BASIC as described in this book, you will have little trouble adapting most BASIC programs to your computer.

One other popular version of Microsoft BASIC is discussed in this book, that supplied with the Radio Shack TRS-80 Model III. This version is compared with BASIC-80, allows you to see some typical variations from BASIC-80.

To give credit where credit is due, Microsoft did not invent BASIC. This was accomplished by Prof. John G. Kemeny and Prof. Thomas E. Kurtz, who originally designed, implemented and introduced BASIC at Dartmouth College in 1964. BASIC was then implemented on many large computers before hobby computers and Microsoft came along.

There are many other languages available for microcomputers, among them FORTRAN, LISP, C, COBOL, FORTH and Pascal. However, BASIC is the most popular, and most of the programs listed in the many hobby computer magazines are in BASIC.

There are many ways to program computers: in machine language, in assembly language and in high-level languages. Machine language and assembly language (low-level languages) require an intimate knowledge of how your specific computer works. Generally such programs are not transportable. That is, an assembly language program for an Apple will not run on a TRS-80. However, BASIC is a high-level language and it is transportable. A BASIC program written for an Apple will probably run on a TRS-80, with a few slight changes.

A high-level language must be either compiled or interpreted. An interpreter is easier to work with, but a compiled language will usually run the program faster. Most languages are either compiled or interpreted, but not both. An advantage of BASIC is that it can be run either way. That is, frequently a BASIC compiler is offered for a given computer, in addition to the BASIC interpreter. Microsoft offers a compiler for BASIC-80 and TRS-80 BASIC. This compiler is described in Chapter 10 in this book. That chapter also explains in more detail the differences between a compiler and an interpreter. However, the main thrust of this book is on interpreted BASIC, which is what you will most likely be using.

I think you will find programming in BASIC an easy-to-learn, fascinating hobby. The challenges are many, and you will continue to learn more and more about the subtle techniques of advanced BASIC programming as your experience grows. I've been programming in Microsoft BASIC for over eight years and I'm still discovering new tricks of the trade.

Have fun!

Ken Knecht
Yuma, AZ

Chapter One

Definitions

Before we get into programming, it would probably be best to present a glossary of the terms used in this book. This will include some sample commands to illustrate certain points and provide an insight into the way BASIC works. Any commands mentioned in this chapter will be explained in detail in later chapters, so do not despair if the operation or use of a command mentioned is not clearly explained. Also, the bracketed designations of which versions of BASIC support the command will not be used in this chapter.

Terms will be defined in an order which permits later definitions to use terms defined earlier. Therefore, they are not in alphabetical order.

INITIALIZATION: This is the process of loading the BASIC interpreter into memory and defining the parameters in which it will operate.

Details of this process vary considerably depending on the operating system used, so it will be left to you to use the method described in your documentation.

COMMAND: These are instructions to BASIC that are generally, but not necessarily, used in direct mode. By direct mode we mean a command used to operate BASIC directly, without writing a program. When BASIC is ready to accept a command (not running a program) it displays OK (sometimes a > or other prompt is used). This is called command mode. Here's a quick example. After BASIC displays OK, respond with

PRINT 4 + 4

This causes BASIC to display 8 and then display the prompt. This is a command. If you entered

    10 PRINT 4 + 4

nothing would happen immediately. If you then entered RUN on the next line BASIC would then display 8, then the prompt OK again. In this case

    10 PRINT 4 + 4

is a BASIC program. The line number 10 preceding the word PRINT makes it a program line, and the RUN command must be used to execute the program; BASIC will not print the answer to 4 + 4 until you enter RUN.

Any instruction to BASIC not preceded by a line number is a command, and will be executed at once. Any instruction preceded by a line number is not a command and will not be acted upon until the program is run. Most instructions can be used either way.

STATEMENT: This is any instruction to BASIC preceded by a line number (see LINE NUMBER). Almost all statements can be used as either commands or statements, depending on whether or not a line number is present.

Normally a statement is an instruction that appears in a program while a command is an instruction used in direct mode (see COMMAND). A statement in a program is said to be in the indirect mode. As mentioned earlier, most instructions can be used either way.

LINE NUMBER: This is a number from 0 to 65529 which appears before each statement in a BASIC program. Some utility programs have problems when you use line number 0, so you might want to avoid using this line number.

Program statements will be executed in ascending numerical order, though they do not need to be entered this way. For example, we write the program

    10 A = 4
    20 B = 5
    30 C = A + B
    40 PRINT "FINISHED"

This will add 4 and 5, just as you requested, then print
FINISHED on the terminal. Unfortunately, only the computer
knows how much 4 + 5 is; we forgot to tell it to display the
answer. So we enter

```
35 PRINT C
```

This adds line 35 to the program, between line 30 and line 40,
and the answer (9) will now be printed. Since 35 is greater
than 30, the computer will calculate the answers in lines 10,
20, and 30. Then it will go to the next line number, 35, even
though it was entered after line 40. The program will now
display a 9 before it goes to line 40 and displays FINISHED.

So we see the computer will operate on the lines in numerical order, even if we didn't enter them in that order. You can
see now why we leave some unused numbers between line
numbers, for cases like this. There will be times, not often I
hope, when you will wish you had left more than 9 unused
line numbers. Later we will see how the renumber command
can solve this difficulty.

As we stated earlier, the line numbers can be most any we
wish. For example

```
0 A = 4
100 B = 5
1017 C = A + B
3462 PRINT C
65529 PRINT "FINISHED"
```

This will perform exactly like the preceding program. BASIC
just takes the line numbers in ascending order. It doesn't care
how many numbers we leave out between them. However,
normal programming practice starts the program at line 10
and uses increments of 10 for the following line numbers.

CONSTANT: This is a number used in a program or command. In the previous programs, 4 and 5 were constants. It is
a number that the computer accepts as a value in a program; it
cannot be changed by the program. The range of acceptable
numbers is from 10^{-38} to 10^{+38}. That is, from a number preceded by a decimal point followed by 37 0's to a number
followed by 38 0's. For those not familiar with scientific nota-

tion, 1×10^5 is the same as 100000 and 2×10^{-8} is the same as .00000002. In BASIC we would enter these numbers as 1E5 or 2E – 8.

VARIABLE: This is the symbolic representation of a constant or a number defined by the program. To return to our earlier example

```
10 A = 4
20 B = 5
30 C = A + B
35 PRINT C
40 PRINT "FINISHED"
```

A, B, and C are variables. In this case, A represents the constant 4, B the constant 5, and C represents the program computed values of A + B, or 9. Variables not representing a constant are given a value of 0 until the program sets their values (see CLEAR). The same variable can represent many numbers in the course of a program run. It always holds the last value set, or 0 if no value has yet been set.

In 8K BASIC a variable name may be any length. However, only the first two characters are significant. The first character must be a letter; the second can be a letter or number. In EXTENDED and DISK BASIC 40 characters are significant. The first character must be a letter; the others can be letters, numbers, or decimal points (periods).

Thus, if the following program were run

```
10 HARRY = 1
20 HAROLD = 2
30 PRINT HARRY + HAROLD
```

in 8K BASIC the computer would display a 4, in EXTENDED or DISK BASIC the computer would display a 3. In 8K only the HA would be significant, so line 20 resets HA from 1 to 2, and HA + HA = 4. In DISK or EXTENDED the two variable names are different, so the result is 3.

Do not use FN as the first two characters in a variable unless you mean it to be a user defined function (see the chapter "ARITHMETIC IN BASIC"). See also RESERVED WORDS in this chapter.

ALPHANUMERIC (character): This is any printable character such as A, L, b, &, +, 9, etc. A letter of course is A to Z, a digit (number) from 0 to 9.

CONTROL CHARACTER: This is a special alphanumeric. It is entered by holding the control key down while a character key is pressed. These are used for some special commands to BASIC and should not be used in variables or program names.

NUMERICS: These are numbers. There are several types of numbers used in BASIC.

The INTEGER is a number from −32768 to 32767 with no decimal point. In 8K BASIC this has no special meaning except for the INT( ) function. In the other BASICs integers can be used to decrease the program's running time and save space. This will be discussed further in other chapters.

In EXTENDED and DISK BASIC an integer variable is designated by adding a % to the end of the variable name. Thus A1% is an integer variable.

SINGLE PRECISION is the type of number normally used in BASIC and is assumed unless a number is specifically declared to be an integer or double precision. Single precision numbers have a precision of 7 digits. Therefore,

```
10 A = 1.23456789
20 PRINT A
```

would display 1.23457.

```
10 A = 123456789
20 PRINT A
```

would display 1.23457E + 08.

```
10 A = 999999
20 PRINT A
```

would display 999999, but any greater number would be transformed to the E format. Thus,

```
10 A = 1000000
20 PRINT A
```

would display 1E + 06. Going to the smaller numbers,

```
10 A = .01
20 PRINT A
```

results in .01 but

```
10 A = .001
20 PRINT A
```

gives 1E − 03. See how it works? The computer gives you back your input if the number is between .01 and 999999, otherwise it uses the E format.

In EXTENDED and DISK BASIC an ! can be appended to the end of the variable name to indicate that it is a single precision variable, A1! for example. Normally, however, A1 would be used instead.

DOUBLE PRECISION is found in EXTENDED and DISK BASIC. This format permits 17 digits of precision. The value .01 is still the smallest that can be displayed without going to the E format.

A double precision variable is signified by following the variable name with a #. Thus A1# is a double precision variable.

FLOATING POINT means using the E format mentioned earlier.

STRING: This is a group of alphanumeric characters surrounded by double quotes (" "). Thus, the "FINISHED" of our first example is a string. Strings may be up to 255 characters in length, not including the double quote (" ").

STRING VARIABLE: This is any legal variable name followed by a $. String variables can be used in any version of BASIC. For example,

```
10 A$ = "FINISHED"
20 PRINT A$
```

would result in FINISHED being displayed. Note that the string must be enclosed in double quotes. Thus, strings cannot include a double quote. Later we will see how we can get around this shortcoming. The surrounding double quotes are not displayed with the string.

See CLEAR for more information about strings.

STRING LITERAL: This is the string enclosed by double quotes. A string can include punctuation, numerals, letters, or anything but a quotation mark. Control characters can be included in a string, but as these are invisible it is best not to use them unless you have to.

EXPRESSION: An expression is two or more variables connected with (an) operator(s). Thus, A + B is an expression.

FUNCTION CALL: This is an intrinsic function of BASIC such as SQR(4), which means find the square root of 4. There are many other functions which will be presented in later chapters.

OPERATOR: This is the +, −, ( ), <>, =, etc., used in a statement or command. Many are used and will be detailed in later chapters.

INTRINSIC FUNCTION: This is the same as a function call, mentioned earlier.

ERROR messages: These are displayed by BASIC when you do something you shouldn't. Dividing by 0, asking for the square root of a negative number, making a syntax error such as X)5 instead of X = 5, or many other errors result in error messages. Your BASIC documentation gives a long list of all error messages and their causes. See also Appendix C.

EDIT: This can have two meanings. There is a simple editing which permits you to reenter or change a character while still typing a line (in direct or indirect mode). Another edit feature, only in EXTENDED and DISK BASIC, permits you to return to a program line and replace or insert one or more characters in that line.

RESERVED WORDS: These are used as instructions to BASIC. A reserved word, such as PRINT, cannot be used as a variable in any version of BASIC. In 8K BASIC a reserved word may not be imbedded in a variable name. Thus a variable name such as APRINT or TOTAL would be illegal in 8K BASIC (APRINT contains the reserved word PRINT, TOTAL contains the reserved word TO). A list of reserved words for each version of BASIC is in Appendix B.

SUBROUTINE: This is a part of a program that will be repeated one or more times. It is usually set off from the rest of the program by using higher line numbers than the rest of the program and ends with a RETURN statement. It is used so a sequence of identical statements will not have to be entered several times. This also saves the memory required to contain the additional copies of those same statements.

I/O: This means input/output and refers to the transfer of information to or from the terminal, disk, tape, or other peripheral devices. Input/output is regulated by computer hardware modules, such as the I/O board (terminal), controller (disk), and other modules such as music boards, etc.

DISK: In this book, disk refers to a floppy disk drive. This is a peripheral that uses a round flexible diskette (like a sheet of audio tape) in a sleeve and permits quick random access to the contents for recording or playback. There are many different sizes and configurations of floppy disk drives available. Also, there are hard disks with greatly increased storage area. However, in this book disk refers to the disk system designed for your computer and provided as a normal peripheral.

CASSETTE TAPE: In this book this term and the word *tape* will refer to the standard type 1/8" audio tape cassette and recorder/player used to record and play back programs and data. Special computer controlled cassette machines that use digital recording techniques and other tape formats are also available but are beyond the scope of this book.

DATA: This is any information which is operated on by a program. It is sometimes a large block of numeric or string information typed directly into the program. Data can also be stored on tape or disk and requested by the program when needed.

ARRAY: This is a list of numbers or strings stored in a single variable name; a subscript appended to the variable name is used to access the specific number or string required. (see SUBSCRIPT)

SUBSCRIPT: This is an indicator for a specific element in an array. Thus the array A(10) can hold eleven specific elements of data by calling them A(0) through A(10). Each element of the array holds a specific piece of data (see chapter "ARRAYS AND FILES") with the subscripts uniquely identifying each one.

FILES: These are groups of data, usually related, gathered under a common heading (or name) called the FILE name. Files created and stored on tape or disk can be retrieved and updated or used as data when required. See chapters "ARRAYS AND FILES" and "THE DISK".

SEQUENTIAL FILES: These are files with the items stored as a long continuous stream of data. Sequential files can only be accessed in the order the data was originally stored. You can't skip around from place to place in the file. A single item of data cannot be added, deleted, or replaced without rerecording the entire file.

RANDOM (ACCESS) FILES: These are files of items; each item or group of related items can be stored in a record. Records can be individually accessed in any order and a record or part of a record can be added, replaced or changed at any time.

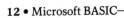

Chapter Two

Getting Started

At long last we will begin to discuss the actual programming in BASIC. In this chapter we will cover the most fundamental statements and commands.

THE NEW COMMAND

If we are going to write a program, the first step is to enter the command NEW (8K). This command erases any program already in memory so we can enter our new program. To use this command, we type in NEW on the next line after we get a prompt, normally OK, from BASIC. (If your BASIC prompt is different from OK, just mentally substitute your prompt whenever I mention the OK prompt, OK?) The OK means BASIC is ready and waiting for our next command. Each command and statement is always followed by a CR (carriage return) to let BASIC know we finished that line of input. Some computers use ENTER or some other word for their carriage return key. We'll continue to call it CR, whatever its name might be on your system.

After the CR, BASIC will reply OK to let you know it has completed the command. In this case it has erased any old program in memory. Actually the program is not erased; all BASIC does is set the address of the end of the old program to the same address as the beginning of the old program, effectively ignoring any program present.

You must type in NEW before entering a new program, or the lines you type in will be added to the old program. Be sure to remember this; if you forget you may be in for a very frustrating experience trying to separate old program lines from new program lines so you can delete them. Throughout the book we will assume NEW was entered prior to entering a new program.

THE CLEAR STATEMENT

The CLEAR statement is used to reset variables and to control program memory allocation. The first statement in the new program should be CLEAR (8K). This sets all variables to 0. It can also allocate space to hold stack variables and set the highest memory address used by BASIC. For example,

    10 CLEAR,64000,5000

would clear all the variables, set the highest memory address used by BASIC to 64000, and set aside 5000 bytes for stack space. If you used

    10 CLEAR,,50

you would not set the top of memory, and you would set aside 50 bytes for stack space. If you used

    10 CLEAR,60000

you would set the top of memory to 60000 and you would set aside 1000 bytes or 1/8 of available free memory, whichever is larger, for stack space. Finally,

    10 CLEAR

would not set the top of memory and would set the stack space to 1000 bytes or 1/8 of free memory, whichever is larger.

In some older versions of Microsoft BASIC, the CLEAR statement was used to allocate string space (rather than stack space) and to set the top of memory. The release 5.0 and later versions operate as described in this section. Check your BASIC manual to verify how CLEAR works on your version.

As we mentioned in the last chapter, each line must begin with a number between 0 and 65529. Line numbers can be entered in any order, and BASIC will execute them in ascending order. Normal program practice is to start with line number 10 and increment each succeeding number by 10 to leave room to add lines later, if necessary. In all the above examples the line number is 10.

If two or more lines with the same number were typed in, the last line entered would be the one accepted by BASIC. Thus, to change a line all you need do is enter another line with the same line number. To delete a line just enter its line number with nothing following it. Careful, it's easy to do by mistake.

Each line entered must end with a CR. BASIC will add the line feed to move down to the next line.

After a line is entered (a line number followed by a statement followed by a CR) you will not get an OK from BASIC. This saves time when entering multiple lines. However, the OK is implied, and we can enter a command at any time instead of the next line. In some versions of Microsoft BASIC, for example the version on the TRS-80, a prompt is given after every line is entered. (From now on, in examples where there could be confusion as to who typed what, the user input will be underlined.)

```
NEW
OK
10 CLEAR
NEW
OK
```

The second entry of NEW erased the line (10 CLEAR). We could also erase it by entering 10 followed by a CR. Line number 10 followed by another statement would erase the original line 10 and replace it with a new line 10. For example,

```
10 CLEAR
10 CLEAR,,1000
```

would replace 10 CLEAR with 10 CLEAR,,1000.

THE LET STATEMENT

The next statement is LET. This statement is probably used more than any other but you will rarely see LET in a program. We'll explain that bit of nonsense in a moment.

The LET (8K) statement is an assignment statement. It is used to assign a value to a variable. Thus:

```
20 LET A = 10
30 LET B = 20
```

Here we have assigned the constant 10 to variable A and 20 to variable B. So if we put in line 40

```
40 LET C = A + B
```

C will have a 30 (A + B or 10 + 20) assigned to it. The = in the LET statement can be confusing. Normally we understand it to show equality (4 = 2 + 2). We can use it with this meaning in BASIC but can also say

```
40 LET B = B + A
```

In math this would make no sense; but in BASIC it means "LET the new value of B be equal to the old value of B plus the value of A". This is a perfectly legal statement in BASIC and you will use it often. Also, the fewer variable names you use, the faster the program will run and the less memory it will need to store the variables.

To give another example, you cannot say

```
40 LET A + B = C
```

BASIC doesn't solve equations of this type. You can only have one variable to the left of the equal (=) sign.

For another example, consider

```
10 LET A = 10
20 LET B = 20
30 LET C + A = 40
```

Again this would not be legal. There is more than a single variable to the left of the equal (=) sign. You must be consistent and say

30 LET C = 40 − A

Any variables appearing on the right of the equal (=) sign would normally have been assigned values, but if not, the value would be 0. Attempting to divide by a variable that has not been assigned a value is the same a dividing by 0, and dividing by 0 is illegal (the result would be infinity).

If you have a situation in a program where division by 0 takes place, the error message DIVISION BY ZERO is displayed and BASIC produces machine infinity (approximately 1E + 38) as the result of the computation and goes on with the program. If the evaluation of an exponentiation results in 0 being raised to a negative power, the same result occurs.

Finally, why do you rarely see LET in a program? That's because you do not need to write the LET in a LET statement. For example,

10 A = 10

is the same as writing

10 LET A = 10

You will normally assign variables without the LET to save typing time and computer memory. That's why I mentioned earlier that you'll rarely see the word LET in a program. Be aware, however, that the program will run slightly faster if the LET is included in the LET statements.

THE PEEK AND POKE STATEMENTS

The PEEK (8K) statement is a special kind of assignment statement. It can be used to assign to a variable the value of data stored in any memory location. For example, the statement

10 A = PEEK(120)

would assign to variable A the contents of memory location 120. This would be a data byte from 0 to 255. A PEEK is normally used to move a machine language program from one area to another, to return a value generated by a machine language program (see USR and CALL statements), or to examine the contents of some special system memory locations (like a clock or timer).

The POKE statement (8K) is the opposite of PEEK. It is used to place the value of a variable into a specific memory location. It, too, is frequently used with machine language programs.

The POKE statement is used as follows:

```
10 POKE 10426,142
```

This would put the byte 142 (must be less than 256) in memory location 10426. The values used with PEEK and POKE can be variables.

```
10 POKE A, B
```

The memory location must be 32767 or less in 8K, up to 65536 in the other versions. In 8K you can use a number larger than 32767 by subtracting 65536 from it and using the resulting negative number as the address. Thus I=PEEK (40000−65536). As you become more proficient in BASIC you will discover many more uses for these statements.

THE PRINT STATEMENT

This statement is used to direct the computer to display information to the user. It can be used for many things.

```
10 A = 10
20 B = 20
30 C = A + B
```

Now only the computer knows what the answer is. To have it tell us, we need to add line 40.

```
40 PRINT C
```

Now when the program reaches line 40 it will print 30. But by then we may have forgotten what the 30 represents. So we can change line 40 to

```
40 PRINT "THE ANSWER IS";C
```

Essentially, what we have done is to tell the computer to print the string "THE ANSWER IS" followed by the value of the variable C, which is 30. Anything enclosed in quotes (" ") after the word PRINT will be displayed by the computer. The semicolon (;) following the quoted words tells BASIC that the next thing displayed should follow immediately on the same line. Thus C, which follows the semicolon (;), will be displayed. Since the C is not surrounded by quotes, BASIC will assume C is a variable and print whatever value is stored in that variable, in this case 30. So we would get

```
THE ANSWER IS 30
```

BASIC always skips a space (or inserts a space if you prefer) before and after a positive number (stored in a variable). This is the reason we get the space between the word from the string, IS, and the first digit of the value in C, the 3. However, if the 30 were negative, we'd get

```
THE ANSWER IS-30
```

To get around this we could change line 40 to

```
40 PRINT "THE ANSWER IS ";C
```

Note the space between IS and the closing quote. Then the computer would print

```
THE ANSWER IS  30
```

or

```
THE ANSWER IS  -30
```

Note that the computer does not print the variable C as C because it has no quotes. If we wrote

40 PRINT "THE ANSWER IS";"C"

the computer would print

THE ANSWER ISC

Perhaps by now we have forgotten what the answer really represents. So,

40 PRINT "THE SUM OF";A;"PLUS";B;" = ";C;"."

This would print as

THE SUM OF 10 PLUS 20 = 30.

Note that we put the semicolon (;) between each item we wanted printed, so each item would follow the previous item on the same line. To write it another way to make this point clearer,

40 PRINT "THE SUM OF";
50 PRINT A;
60 PRINT "PLUS";
70 PRINT B;
80 PRINT " = ";C;"."

would print

THE SUM OF 10 PLUS 20 = 30.

However, if we changed line 50 to

50 PRINT A

we'd get

THE SUM OF 10
PLUS 20 = 30.

Since there was no semicolon (;) after the A, BASIC started a new line of printing after it printed the value of A, or 10. Let's try another.

```
10 PRINT "THE ANSWER";
20 PRINT "IS"
```

This would result in

```
THE ANSWERIS
```

because we put no space before IS or after ANSWER. To correct this

```
20 PRINT " IS"
```

so

```
THE ANSWER IS
```

would result.

BASIC only adds spaces before and after a positive number, not a string. So

```
30 PRINT "IS";"40"
```

would give us

```
THE ANSWER IS40
```

because we left out the space after IS or before 40. Because the 40 was a string literal (string between quotes) and not a variable, the space was not added to the number by BASIC.

You can now see how we can put together long sequences of string literals intermixed with variables and separated by semicolons to print out one long output line. Don't forget to put each string literal in quotes and add a space within the quotes, if necessary, for desired spacing.

Note also in the last line 30 we didn't put a semicolon (;) after the 40. This is so the next print statement will start on the next line.

There is another divider we can use in the PRINT statement besides the semicolon (;). That is the comma (,). We noted the semicolon causes no spacing between outputs. The comma works differently. It causes the line to be divided into 14-character zones. The comma in a PRINT statement causes the item appearing after the comma to start at the beginning of the next zone. Thus,

```
10 PRINT "A","B","TOTAL"
20 A = 10
30 B = 20
40 C = A + B
50 PRINT A,B,C
```

results in

```
A    B    TOTAL
10   20   30
```

In line 10, A is followed by a comma, which means that the next item printed will start in the next zone, 14 spaces over from the beginning of the last zone, and so on. See Figure 2-1. The same applies to line 50. We didn't put a comma (or semicolon) after TOTAL in line 10 because we wanted line 50 to start a new line. You can mix commas and semicolons in a PRINT statement. If you use them together the comma will over-ride the semicolon.
The semicolon in

```
50 PRINT A,B;C
```

would make sense. But in

```
50 PRINTA,B,;C
```

it would not: the semicolon would be ignored.
Of course, the semicolon between the B and C in the first line 50 would not give us the display we want; we want C to be printed under TOTAL, not right after B.
You will find the comma spacing very useful for printing tables in BASIC. Remember, a comma doesn't give you 14 spaces after the previous item; it starts 14 spaces after the

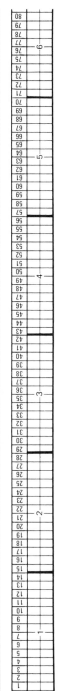

Figure 2-1. Using commas in a PRINT statement causes the line to be divided into 14-character zones.

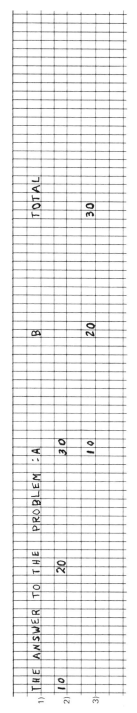

```
1) THE ANSWER TO THE PROBLEM : A              B              TOTAL

2)        10              20              30

3)                        10              20              30
```

Figure 2-2. To align columns, put the appropriate number of commas in the PRINT statement where they are needed.

1) Heading
2) PRINT A,B,C
3) PRINT,,A,B,C

beginning of the previous item (assuming the previous item started at the beginning of a print zone). If the previous item is more than 15 characters long, the next item still starts at the beginning of the next print zone (or next line if no more print zones).

```
10 PRINT"THE ANSWER TO THE PROBLEM:","A","B",
   "TOTAL"
50 PRINT A,B,C
```

would give you

```
THE ANSWER TO THE PROBLEM:  A       B       TOTAL
10      20      30
```

This is not what we had in mind. Figure 2-2 illustrates the spacing. To correct this use

```
50 PRINT,,A,B,C
```

This would skip two print zones (two commas after PRINT) and then print A, B, and C as we wish.:

```
THE ANSWER TO THE PROBLEM:  A       B       TOTAL
                            10      20      30
```

So we see we can put several commas together to move items to the correct column.

When entering programs, PRINT can be replaced with a ?. So

```
60 ? "THE ANSWER IS"
```

is the same as

```
60 PRINT "THE ANSWER IS"
```

This can save a lot of typing. Also, PRINT or ? on a line by itself,

```
70 PRINT
```

or

70 ?

both cause the computer to skip a line. This is useful for putting blank lines in your display.

So much for PRINT, for the moment. We'll see more uses for PRINT as the book proceeds.

THE REM STATEMENT

The REM (8K) statement is an easy one. Anything we type after REM (for *remark*) is ignored by BASIC. Thus we can use REM to annotate the program and help us remember what we were accomplishing with that statement. What was very clear and obvious when we write the code might not be so clear when we are debugging the program later, and even less clear when we decide to make some changes to the program six months or a year down the line. The only disadvantage to using REM is that it uses valuable memory. To give a trivial example:

```
10 A = 10
20 B = 20
30 REM THE A AND B ARE THE NUMBERS TO BE ADDED
40 C = A + B REM "C" IS THE TOTAL
```

We can put a REM after a statement or on a line by itself. We can put quotes, commas, semicolons, or whatever we wish in a REM statement. BASIC leaves the REM in the program but does not look at the material following it. If we said

```
40 REM "C" IS THE TOTAL C = A + B
```

BASIC would ignore the C = A + B. All operable statements must be placed before the REM. In EXTENDED the REM can be replaced with an apostrophe. Thus:

```
40 C = A + B ' "C" IS THE TOTAL
```

SIMPLE EDITING

When typing in a program or command you might accidentally type the wrong character or characters. Rather than retype the whole line you can edit it. For example, in the line

10 PRINS

we meant, of course, to type a T instead of the S. To correct this, press the rubout (sometimes other names are used, such as delete) key. This will delete the last character and place it between backslashes(/). Each time you press rubout you delete the next undeleted character. To replace a deleted character(s) just type it (them) in normal order. Generally this method is used when a hardcopy terminal is used. If you are using a CRT for display, then the control-H is used. It simply erases the last entered character from the screen. Each additional control-H deletes the last character in the line. To replace deleted characters just start typing again. What you see is what you will get.

To delete the whole line use control-U. The cursor or printhead will do a CR LF (carriage return-line feed sequence) and the line will be deleted, although you may still see it on your terminal.

Note that these methods of editing must be used before the final CR is entered at the end of the line. Once the line is entered with the CR you can only replace the entire line by repeating the line number and reentering the entire line. (If you have EXTENDED or DISK BASIC see the chapter on editing. This will permit you to change only part of a previously entered line.)

THE INPUT STATEMENT

INPUT (8K) is a very useful command. It is used to get data from the operator while the program is running.

```
10 INPUT A
20 INPUT B
30 C = A + B
40 PRINT "THE ANSWER IS";C
```

This program will print a ? on the terminal when it reaches line 10. The operator would then type a response, let's say a 60, followed by the usual CR to tell the computer the end of the input data has been reached. As all entered information must end in a CR (except when using the INKEY$ command) from now on we will assume you will do that so we don't have to write it every time.

Line 20 would also display a ?; you could enter a 40 here. Then the program would display

```
THE ANSWER IS 100
```

So you could enter any data you wished for A and B in this way. If you wanted to be more specific you could add

```
5 PRINT "THE FIRST NUMBER TO BE ADDED"
15 PRINT "THE SECOND NUMBER TO BE ADDED"
```

This would prompt the operator so he or she would know what the program expected. If you ran the program as written, the ? would be on the line following the prompt. If you added a ; to the end of lines 5 and 15, the question mark would follow the prompt. The letter (variable name) following the INPUT is the variable which will be assigned the entered input value. So line 10 assigns the value entered to A, line 20 assigns the value entered to B.

We could write the program in a different way.

```
10 PRINT "TYPE IN THE TWO NUMBERS TO BE ADDED"
20 INPUT A,B
30 C = A + B
40 PRINT "THE ANSWER IS";C
```

This would type the prompt, then a ? on the next line. If you entered 40, 60 the program would go on to line 30. However, if you typed 40 only, the program would print ?REDO FROM START on the next line to tell you that you did not enter the proper data; in this case the number of data items was not correct. If you entered 40, 60, 80 BASIC would again display ?REDO FROM START to tell you that the input was not correct. One more possibility: if you typed A,B instead of numbers you'd get the usual ?REDO FROM START. BASIC expected numbers, not string input, so it requested you to do it over.

You can put as many variables after an INPUT statement as you wish to have entered. As described above, be sure the operator knows how many items are required.

When inputting values you must put a comma between each number in the input variable list, or BASIC will consider it a single number. So answering 40 60 instead of 40,60 would result in BASIC assigning 4060 to variable A and returning a ?REDO FROM START because it did not see any data for variable B. (Note that the comma is used here in a way which is completely unrelated to its use in a PRINT statement.)

In 8K, INPUT is illegal in the direct (command) mode.

You can put your prompt string directly in the INPUT statement; you don't have to use a separate PRINT statement as we have shown so far.

```
10 INPUT "TWO NUMBERS TO ADD";A,B
20 C = A + B
30 PRINT "THE ANSWER IS";C
```

Essentially, it is just the INPUT statement with a PRINT statement built into it. The ? is automatically added to the prompt string so you would get

```
TWO NUMBERS TO ADD?
```

from line 10. Otherwise the same rules as for the plain INPUT statement hold true.

If you should wish to print the included prompt without the trailing question mark, just use a comma instead of a semicolon after the prompt string. Thus changing line 10 to

```
10 INPUT "ENTER TWO NUMBERS TO ADD",A,B
```

would result in

```
ENTER TWO NUMBERS TO ADD
```

from line 10.

The INPUT statement can also be used for entering strings as well as numbers. In the chapter "DEFINITIONS" we mentioned string variables. These are variable names followed by a $, as in A$ or A1$. We could enter a number in a string variable, but it would be treated as a string, not a number. For example:

```
10 INPUT "YOUR NAME";A$
20 PRINT "HELLO ";A$
```

Let's explore a few possibilities using this little program.

```
RUN
YOUR NAME?   JOHN
HELLO JOHN
OK
```

The computer accepts your input of JOHN and prints it in line 20. Another example.

```
RUN
YOUR NAME? .007
HELLO .007
OK
```

The computer accepted your input of .007 as a word, not a number, so it displayed .007. If the variable had been A instead of A$, the computer would have converted the .007 to the E format and displayed

```
HELLO 7E – 03
```

(See NUMBERS in the DEFINITIONS chapter.) Another example:

```
RUN
YOUR NAME? JONES, JOHN
?REDO FROM START
YOUR NAME? JONES
HELLO JONES
OK
```

The reason for the error message was that BASIC was looking for a single string to store in A$ and was given two strings, JONES and JOHN. Remember, the comma separates items entered in response to the INPUT statement. However, if you used

```
RUN
YOUR NAME? JOHN JONES
HELLO JOHN JONES
OK
```

But what if you wanted to include the comma?

```
RUN
YOUR NAME? "JONES, JOHN"
HELLO JONES, JOHN
OK
```

Using the quotation marks included the comma in the string. So if we wish to include a comma, in an address perhaps, we'd enclose our response in quotation marks.

As with numbers, we can ask for two or more strings in a single INPUT statement.

```
NEW
OK
10 PRINT "WHAT CITY AND STATE DO YOU LIVE IN?"
20 INPUT A$,B$
30 PRINT A$;", ";B$
RUN
WHAT CITY AND STATE DO YOU LIVE IN?
? BOULDER CITY, COLORADO
BOULDER CITY, COLORADO
OK
```

Note the ", " between the A$ and the B$ in line 30. This is to put a comma followed by a space between the two strings.

If you answered

```
RUN
WHAT CITY AND STATE DO YOU LIVE IN?
```

```
? BOULDER CITY
?REDO FROM START
? BOULDER CITY, COLORADO
BOULDER CITY, COLORADO
OK
```

BASIC wanted two strings but you only supplied one the first time. If you replied

```
RUN
WHAT CITY AND STATE DO YOU LIVE IN?
? "CHICAGO, ILL."
?REDO FROM START
? CHICAGO, ILL.
CHICAGO, ILL.
OK
```

Since you used the quotation marks, BASIC disregarded the comma within the quotes and took your reply to be a single string.

You can mix string and numeric data in an INPUT statement.

```
NEW
OK
10 INPUT "YOUR AGE AND PLACE OF BIRTH";A,A$
20 PRINT A;"!! THAT'S OLD! DID ";A$;" EXIST THEN?"
RUN
YOUR AGE AND PLACE OF BIRTH? 19, CHICAGO
19 !! THAT'S OLD! DID CHICAGO EXIST THEN?
OK
```

Note where the spaces are strategically located: after DID and before EXIST.

THE LINE INPUT STATEMENT

If you wish to enter a string containing one or more commas in reply to an INPUT request without using the quotation marks, you can use LINE INPUT (EXTENDED). Since this occurs in EXTENDED BASIC, the input string can be up to 255 characters long. Note this INPUT statement is only used for string input; no numbers are allowed. It is used the same way as the INPUT statement except no question mark is printed and commas are ignored. So if we change lines 20 and 30 to

```
20 LINE INPUT A$
30 PRINT A$
```

the result would be

```
RUN
WHAT CITY AND STATE DO YOU LIVE IN?
NEW PALTZ, NY
NEW PALTZ, NY
OK
```

The comma was ignored and NEW PALTZ, NY was accepted as a single string. You can use LINE INPUT for whole sentences, multiple words, or whatever you wish. Only a CR ends the string. If we changed line 10 to

```
10 PRINT "WHAT CITY AND STATE DO YOU LIVE IN? ";
```

and ran the program, we'd get

```
WHAT CITY AND STATE DO YOU LIVE IN? LIMA, OHIO
LIMA, OHIO
OK
```

Note the added space after the question mark and the semicolon added to the end of the line. As with the INPUT statement, the prompt can be included in the LINE INPUT statement.

```
NEW
OK
10 LINE INPUT "YOUR CITY AND STATE? ";A$
20 PRINT A$
RUN
YOUR CITY AND STATE? ONEONTA, NY
ONEONTA, NY
OK
```

Don't forget to add your own question mark, if desired, and a space after the prompt string to make things look pretty.

MULTIPLE STATEMENTS IN A LINE

The next new feature is the use of the colon (:). This handy BASIC punctuation permits putting more than one statement in a line.

```
10 A = 10 : B = 20 : C = A + B
20 PRINT C
```

In fact, we could even have added the contents of line 20 to line 10 by using another : .

We can put any number of statements up to 72 characters (including spaces) in a single line in 8K BASIC; in EXTENDED BASIC we can enter up to 255 characters in a line. In EX-TENDED BASIC we can also use the line feed key to break the physical lines into logical lines. Each line feed starts any following characters on the next line. You are still limited to 255 characters (each line feed also counts as a character) per line.

How can we enter a 255 character line when we have an 80 character per line terminal? We have two choices; use line feeds as mentioned in the previous paragraph, or just keep typing and let BASIC insert an automatic CR LF sequence when the end of the line on the terminal is reached. See the WIDTH command for more details. In 8K BASIC we have no choice but the second. Here's an example of using line feeds in a line. We'll use /LF/ to indicate pressing the line feed key.

```
10 A = 10 : B = 20 : C = 30 : D = 40 : E = 50 : F = 60 /LF/
   G = A + B : H = C + D : I = E + F
20 PRINT G,H,I
```

Note how we can add spaces after the /LF/ to bring the G under the A as shown. This isn't necessary but makes the program look nicer when it's printed out (see LIST).

You can use LPRINT to PRINT on your line printer. This works the same as PRINT. LPRINT assumes your line printer can print a 132 character line. See WIDTH command to change this.

THE END STATEMENT

Well, enough printing and input for the moment. Next we'll mention the END (8K) statement. This statement is usually optional. If used, it is placed at the end of the program. Sometimes it is required. For example, in a conditional statement (next chapter) it might be used as one of the conditions. If subroutines are used (next chapter) and they follow the main program, you might need to use an END to keep the program from running into the subroutines when it shouldn't. This will make more sense after you have read the next chapter and seen some examples.

When BASIC gets to the END statement it stops the program and prints OK.

THE STOP STATEMENT

STOP (8K) is generally used for a temporary stop in a program. You can put it anywhere in the program. It is usually used for debugging a program. When BASIC sees STOP it displays BREAK IN LINE XX, where XX is the line number containing the STOP, followed by the usual OK. To continue the program after a STOP has been reached just type in CONT (8K) (for *continue*). CONT could also be used after an END. However, if you change a program line you can't use CONT. However, you can display variables and/or change them and still successfully use CONT.

THE LIST COMMAND

The LIST (8K) command is used to display all or part of the program. For instance

```
NEW
10 A = 10 : B = 20
20 ? C
15 C = A + B
LIST
10 A = 10 : B = 20
15 C = A + B
20 PRINT C
OK
```

Note: when the program was listed the lines were put into correct order and the ? was changed to PRINT.

To list only selected lines you have three options. You can use one or two line numbers as follows:

1) LIST 100-200
   LISTS lines 100 to line 200 inclusive.
2) LIST -200
   LISTS from lowest line number to line 200
3) LIST 100-
   LISTS from 100 to the highest line number.

LIST can be used for only a single line in EXTENDED BASIC. Just type in LIST 15 to list only line 15 on the terminal. In 8K if only a single line number is given, that line number and all higher will be listed. This is the same as option 3 above.

You can list on the line printer by using LLIST (EXTENDED) instead of LIST. The LLIST command assumes a line printer width of 132 characters. See the WIDTH command to change this.

THE NULL COMMAND

NULL (8K) is used to add null(s) to the end of each line going to your CRT or hard copy terminal. BASIC just keeps sending characters while your terminal is returning to start a new line after a line has been completed. In some cases the terminal will lose one or more characters because it can't keep up. If this happens you can use NULL to add a few null characters to the end of each line to give the terminal a little extra time. For example, if your terminal runs at 30 CPS you might try

    NULL 2

or

    NULL 3

You'll have to experiment a bit to find the right setting for your terminal. If it is a fast CRT (9600 baud), you won't need any nulls at all. NULL can also be used in a program, but it is generally used as a command at the beginning of an operating session.

THE SWAP STATEMENT

The SWAP (EXTENDED) statement is very handy for moving data between two variables of the same type.

```
NEW
OK
10 A = 10 : B = 20
20 SWAP A,B
30 PRINT A;B
RUN
 20      10
OK
```

As you can see, the contents of variable A were moved to B and vice versa. If you don't have EXTENDED BASIC, the following program does the same thing.

```
NEW
OK
10 A = 10 : B = 20
20 T = A : A = B : B = T
30 PRINT A;B
RUN
 20      10
OK
```

You can't say

```
20 A = B : B = A
```

because then A = B (currently 20) and B = A (20 again). You have to use the extra variable for temporary storage.

THE CONTROL CHARACTERS

There are 10 control characters that BASIC understands. A control character is entered by holding down the control key and at the same time pressing the key associated with it.

control-A   Enters edit mode (EXTENDED) on the line being entered.

control-C	Interrupts program execution and returns to BASIC command level. This can also be used to stop a listing.
control-G	Rings the bell at the terminal.
control-H	Backspace. Deletes the last character typed.
control-I	Tab. Tab stops are every eight columns.
control-O	Halts program output while execution continues. Another control-O restarts output. Any PRINT or LPRINT while output is stopped are gone forever.
control-R	Retypes the line that is currently being typed.
control-S	Suspends program execution. OK is not printed.
control-Q	Resumes program execution after a control-S.
control-U	Deletes the line that is currently being typed.

If you use control-C to stop a program, you can continue at any line in the program by typing GOTO XX where XX is the line number. You can restart the program from the beginning with RUN, or you can resume execution from the point where the program was interrupted by using CONT.

## Chapter Three

Branching and Loops

This chapter presents some of the most useful statements in BASIC. In fact, the ability to branch to different parts of the program depending on the results of operations is what makes a computer so versatile and powerful.

THE GOSUB AND GOTO STATEMENTS

First we'll discuss branching, beginning with the *unconditional branch*. This means the program branches (or jumps) to another part of the program whenever this statement is encountered. There are two types of unconditional branch: the GOTO (8K) and the GOSUB (8K).

```
10 GOTO 1010
```

tells BASIC to branch to program line 1010 and resume execution at that point.

```
10 GOSUB 1010
20 A = 11
```

tells BASIC to branch to program line 1010 and execute statements, line by line, until it gets to a statement that says RETURN (8K). Then BASIC goes back to the line following the GOSUB statement, in this case line 20. It then goes on with the program from there. Here's an example using both statements.

```
10 PRINT "THIS PROGRAM PRINTS THE SUM"
20 PRINT "OF ANY TWO NUMBERS YOU"
30 PRINT "ENTER. TYPE CONTROL-C TO END."
40 PRINT "YOUR NUMBERS? "
50 INPUT A,B
60 GOSUB 80
70 GOTO 40
80 C = A + B
90 PRINT C
100 RETURN
```

This is a trivial example, but it shows how the statements work. Lines 10 through 30 introduce the program. Line 40 is the prompt. Line 50 inputs the two numbers. Line 60 transfers control to the subroutine beginning at line 80. There the program adds the numbers and prints the result. Line 100 causes a return to line 70, which then branches the program to line 40 for another pair of numbers. This will continue until you type control-C.

When using subroutines, always let the subroutine get to the RETURN. Don't use a GOTO to jump out of a subroutine and skip the normal RETURN. If you must use the GOTO to get out of a SUBROUTINE (bad practice) be sure the program still sees a RETURN, as it would have if you had not used the GOTO. If you leave RETURNS hanging and never used, you could run out of memory, since each return address takes up at least two memory locations until it is used.

Normally we would only use a subroutine if it were called from at least two different places in a program. The idea behind using the subroutine is to avoid duplicating a routine in a program. Thus any part of the program that requires that routine can call it with a GOSUB. In some of the early example programs we will be using subroutines merely for the sake of using them, to get you used to seeing and understanding the GOSUB and RETURN statements. In a real program you'd only use a subroutine if it were used by more than one part of a program.

THE IF STATEMENT

The IF (8K) statement is one of the statements that permits *conditional branching*. This means program control only transfers to a line if some condition is fulfilled. Let's say we wanted to display the multiplication tables from 1 to 12 up to x 12. (By the way, the multiplication sign in BASIC is an asterisk (*), as shown in the following program.)

```
10 A = 1 : B = 1
20 GOSUB 60
30 A = A + 1
40 IF A = 13 THEN END
50 GOTO 20
60 C = A*B
70 PRINT A;"X";B;" = ";C
80 B = B + 1
90 IF B = 13 THEN 110
100 GOTO 60
110 B = 1
120 RETURN
```

This program is a bit more complex than some of the previous examples. In line 10 we set A and B to 1. Line 20 transfers control to the subroutine at line 60. There we multiply A and B, and in line 70 we show the results. In line 80 we add 1 to B. Since we only want to multiply to 12, we check B in line 90 to see if it is greater than 12. The IF-THEN statement transfers control to line 110 if B = 13. If B is equal to 13, line 110 resets B to 1, and line 120 RETURNs to line 30 where we add 1 to A. In line 40, we check to see if A is greater than 12. If so, we END and stop the program. If not over 12 we GOTO 20 in line 50 and do it all again.

IF is a conditional branch statement which permits us to determine the order in which program statements are executed. If the condition tested is true, then the action specified takes place. The THEN in an IF statement can be another statement or it can be used to transfer to another program line. If a tested condition results in a 0, the condition is false; any other value, usually − 1, is true. The results of a conditional operator such as a comparison will provide either the − 1 or the 0 response. We will learn more about conditional operators in the next chapter. At this point only the = operator will be considered.

Here are some examples.

```
10 IF A = B THEN 100
20 IF A = B THEN A = 10
30 IF A = B THEN GOSUB 200
40 IF A = B THEN 300 : A = 30
50 IF A = B THEN A = 10 : GOTO 400
```

In line 10 we branch to line 100 if A = B. If A does not equal B then we skip the rest of the statement.

In line 20 if A = B we put 10 in variable A. If not, we skip the rest of the statement.

In line 30 if A = B we do a GOSUB to the subroutine at line 200. If not, we skip the rest of the statement.

In line 40 if A = B we GOTO line 300. If not, we skip the rest of the statement. Note carefully that the A = 30 statement will not be executed in either case; the program will simply transfer to line 300 if A = B.

In line 50, however, if A = B the A = 10 statement will execute; then the GOTO 400 will execute. If A does not equal B we skip both the A = 10 and the GOTO 400. That part of the line will only be executed if the statement is true.

Be careful not to write lines like line 40. This is a very easy mistake to make, especially if there are quite a few statements on the line and the IF statement is not the first one. For example:

```
60 A = 5 : B = 10 : IF C = 20 THEN 40 : GOSUB 100
```

Note again that this does not mean if C does not equal 20 then GOSUB 100. This would be written

```
60 A = 5 : B = 10 : IF C = 20 THEN 40 ELSE GOSUB 100
```

Unfortunately the ELSE clause is only allowed in EX-TENDED and DISK BASIC. If you don't have the ELSE clause you could use

```
60 A = 5 : B = 10 : IF C = 20 THEN 80
70 GOSUB 100 : GOTO 90
80 GOTO 40
90 . . . . . . . .
```

or

```
60 A = 5 : B = 10 : IF C = 20 THEN 40
70 GOSUB 100
```

The second example is easier but the first method must be used sometimes. For example,

```
60 IF A = 30 THEN GOSUB 300 ELSE GOSUB 400
```

would be changed to

```
60 IF A = 30 THEN 80
70 GOSUB 400 : GOTO 90
80 GOSUB 300
90 . . . . . . . .
```

if you were using 8K BASIC.
The ELSE (EXTENDED) version can also be nested.

```
80 IF C = 20 THEN 120 ELSE IF D = 40 THEN IF F = 10 THEN
   G = 40 ELSE GOSUB 170
```

An ELSE always refers to the most recent unterminated THEN. That is, it refers to the most recent THEN to which an ELSE has not already been assigned. To assign ELSEs to THENs, start at the middle and work out, or start at the ends and work in to the center. If C does not equal 20, D equals 40, and F equals 10, then G equals 40. If D equals 40, and F does not equal 10, and C does not equal 20, then the GOSUB 170 will be executed. If C does not equal 20 and D does not equal 40, then the line will be ignored. If C equals 20, then the program will move to line 120 and the rest of line 80 will be ignored.

Be very careful of your logic when using such complicated statements. When we cover relational and logical statements in the next chapter you will find easier ways to write a statement like the one in line 80. For example, though out of context, here's the same statement using logical operators.

```
80 IF C = 20 THEN 120 ELSE IF D = 40 AND F = 10 THEN G = 40
   ELSE GOSUB 170
```

The IF-THEN-ELSE statement is very powerful. It is especially useful to make the change of a variable's value dependent upon the results of an IF comparison. Here's another example of an IF statement.

```
90 IF A = 10 THEN IF B = 20 THEN PRINT "B = 20 AND A = 10"
   ELSE PRINT "A = 10" ELSE PRINT "A DOES NOT EQUAL 10"
```

THE ON . . . GOTO-GOSUB STATEMENT

The ON . . . GOTO (8K) statement is another useful form of the IF statement. It is used as follows

```
10 ON X GOTO 100,150,200
```

This means if $X = 1$ then GOTO 100, if $X = 2$ then GOTO 150, if $X = 3$ then GOTO 200. X cannot be less than 0 or greater than 255. If X is a decimal number it is truncated to an integer. By truncated, we mean if $X = 2.5$ the ON . . . GOTO considers X to be 2. The actual value of X is not changed; its value is simply evaluated for use in this statement. If $X = 0$ or X is greater than 3 in this example, the ON . . . GOTO statement is skipped and the program goes on to the line following line 10.

But what if X ranges from 4 to 7? We have two ways to handle this.

```
10 ON X GOTO 0,0,0,100,150,200,250
```

or

```
10 ON X - 3 GOTO 100,150,200,250
```

Either is acceptable, though the second is easier to write and is usually used. In the first statement we could use any integers for the first three 0 lines; they would never be executed because of the range of X (4 to 7).

We can also write (8K)

```
10 ON X GOSUB 100,150,200
```

This follows the same rules as for ON . . . GOTO but a GOSUB is executed instead of a GOTO.

THE FOR. . . NEXT STATEMENT

The FOR statement (8K) is used to generate program loops; that is, repeat one or more statements a predetermined number of times. For example:

```
10 FOR X = 1 TO 10
20 PRINT X
30 NEXT X
```

This program will display the digits from 1 to 10. In line 10 we establish the loop by saying X will vary from 1 to 10. In line 20 we print X. In line 30 the NEXT statement adds one to (increments) X and tests it to see if it has exceeded the limit (10 in this case). If not, the program returns to line 20. When X reaches 10, the program stops (or goes on to the line following line 30 if it exists).

Now let's rewrite the multiplication table program shown earlier in this chapter. This time we'll use the FOR. . . NEXT loop instead of the IF statement.

```
10 FOR A = 1 TO 12
20 FOR B = 1 TO 12
30 C = A*B
40 PRINT A;"X";B;" = ";C
50 NEXT B
60 NEXT A
```

This does the same thing as our larger earlier program. Note that we used a loop within a loop. This is called a *nested loop*.

Line 10 sets the range of variable A from 1 to 12; line 20 does the same for B. Line 30 calculates the product of A and B and stores the result in C. Line 40 prints this operation. Line 50 increments B, tests its value, and goes back to line 30 if B is less than 13. When B reaches 13 the program goes on to line 60. Here A is incremented and tested. If A is less than 13 the program goes back to line 20 where B is reset to 1 again and the B loop is run again. If A is greater than 12 the program ends.

There are other versions of the FOR loop we can use. For example,

```
10 FOR A = 1 TO 12 STEP .1
```

The STEP (8K) allows us to use an increment other than 1. In this example A will vary from 1 to 12 in steps of .1 (1, 1.1, 1.2, 1.3, 1.4, . . . 11.9, 12). Another possibility is

```
10 FOR X = 12 TO 1 STEP −1
```

Now A will vary from 12 to 1 in steps of −1 (12, 11, 10, . . .2, 1).

If no STEP value is given, a STEP size of +1 is assumed. We could also write

```
FOR X = 9.2 TO 3.7 STEP −.1
```

or

```
FOR X = 9.2 TO 3.7 STEP −.2
```

In the second case the loop will only go to 3.8 because the next step would be 3.6, which is out of the loop range. The FOR loop can also use variables, such as

```
10 FOR X = Y TO Z STEP A
```

or

```
10 FOR X = Y TO Z + C STEP A + D
```

A program line such as

```
10 FOR S = 1 TO 0
```

will skip the body of the loop because the limit (0) is less than the starting value plus the step (1 + 1 = 2).

A FOR statement must always have a matching NEXT statement, or you will get an error statement from BASIC and the program will stop.

Speaking of error statements, BASIC will always tell you (or at least give you a hint) when it cannot execute a program statement. Consult your documentation and Appendix C for a list of error messages.

When nesting loops, the NEXT statements must occur in the reverse order of the FOR statements. For example:

```
10 FOR A = 1 TO 10
20 FOR B = 1 TO 5
30 FOR C = 1 TO 20
40 D = A + B + C
50 NEXT C
60 NEXT B
70 NEXT A
```

A program such as

```
10 FOR A = 1 TO 10
20 FOR B = 1 TO 5
30 C = A*B
40 NEXT A
50 NEXT B
```

would not be legal and would not run. Lines 40 and 50 need to be exchanged.

A few variations of the NEXT statement are allowable. For example:

```
10 FOR A = 1 TO 10
20 PRINT A
30 NEXT
```

Since the last FOR used A as the loop counter, the NEXT appearing by itself in line 30 is taken to mean NEXT A. This version will also run a slight bit faster, but the program will be a little harder to understand in some cases. Another version of NEXT is

```
10 FOR A = 1 TO 10
20 FOR B = 1 TO 5
30 C = C + A*B
40 NEXT B,A
```

Here's an example of the use of the FOR statement. They say in the year 1627 Manhattan island was purchased for $24. If this was immediately put in a bank in a savings account at 5% interest compounded annually, what would it amount to in 1977? We'll display a cumulative total every 25 years.

```
10 A = 24 : B = 0 : PRINT "YEAR","ACCOUNT TOTAL"
20 FOR Y = 1 TO 14
30 REM NUMBER OF 25 YEAR PERIODS BETWEEN 1627 AND
   1977
40 FOR X = 1 TO 25
50 REM 25 YEAR PERIOD
60 A = A + (A*.05) : B = B + 1
70 REM B IS THE COUNTER TO KEEP TRACK OF THE YEAR
80 NEXT X
90 PRINT 1627 + B, "$";INT((A*100) + 5)/100
100 NEXT Y
```

First of all, note the new function used in line 90. This is the
INT((A*100) + 5)/100. The INT (8K) function means integer.
The integer function returns the nearest whole number less
than or equal to its argument. If the number following INT
were 12.67, INT would return you a 12; that is, the next lower
whole number or integer. If the number were negative such a
– 12.67, you would again get the next whole lower number, or
– 13. In line 90 INT was used to round off the value in A to the
nearest whole cent. For example, if A = 56.4278 we multiply it
by 100 (A*100) to get 5642.78, which is the amount in cents;
we add .5 cent (giving 5643.28), find the integer, or 5643, then
divide by 100 (/) to get the correct rounded result in dollars, or
56.43. (The .5 was added to abide by the normal rules for
rounding off: numbers .50 and above will be represented in
the final answer by the next higher number rather than the
lower one.) Note how the parentheses were used. Values
within the parentheses are calculated first, as in algebra. We
will explain this in detail in the next chapter.

How would you change the program to print out every 10
years instead of every 25? What if you compounded the interest every month? How would you program that? How
much difference would this make after 350 years? Try it!

Here's another example. Let's say we are on a 5 person
bowling team. At the end of the evening's sport we wish to
calculate each bowler's average and the team average.

```
10 E = 0 : FOR X = 1 TO 5
20 PRINT "BOWLER #";X;" 'S SCORES?"
30 INPUT A,B,C
40 D = INT((A + B + C)/3) : E = E + D
```

```
50 PRINT "BOWLER #";X;"'S AVERAGE IS";D
60 NEXT
70 PRINT "TEAM AVERAGE IS";INT (E/5)
```

How could you change this program to also display a yearly average to date? If you are into team bowling and understand handicaps, how would you include the handicaps in the average calculation? How would you have the program generate a new handicap as a result of the evening's bowling? Try it!

THE WHILE. . . WEND STATEMENT

The WHILE (EXTENDED) statement resembles the FOR . . . NEXT statements, but it is more useful in certain situations. As noted earlier, the FOR loop is preset to a definite value. What if you don't know what this value will be when you are writing the program? That's the time to use a WHILE loop. The WHILE Loop continues to run until the condition placed after the word WHILE is false. The word WEND is used to indicate the end of the body of the WHILE loop. WHILE loops can be nested like FOR loops.

We will use two new operators in this program, the < and the >. The < means *less than*; the> means *greater than*.

Let's use a program example. Let's say you borrow $25,000 and make payments every month. How long would it take to pay off the loan? What will you have paid in total including interest? We'll say the monthly payment is $200 and the interest is 9% compounded monthly (.75%). This program will print out yearly results.

```
10 A = 25000 : B = 200 : C = .0075 : D = 0 : E = 0 : F = 0
20 PRINT "YEAR", "INTEREST PAID", "PRINCIPAL REMAINING"
30 WHILE A>0
40 X = 0 : WHILE X<12
50 A = A + A*C - B : E = E + A*C : F = F + 1
60 X = X + 1
70 WEND : D = D + 1
80 PRINT 1982 + D,INT((E*100) + 5)/100, INT((A*100) + 5)/100
90 WEND
100 PRINT 1982 + D + 1, "$;";INT((E*100) + 5)/100, "$";
   INT((A*100) + 5)/100
110 PRINT F;"$200 PAYMENTS FOR A TOTAL OF $";F*B
```

We will end up with a negative balance and an excessive payment total in the final results because we did not calculate the exact final payment. How could you change the program to end up with a $0 balance and calculate the exact amount paid? Try it! In the program, A was used for the running balance to be paid, B for the payment, C for the monthly interest, D for the year counter, E for the running total of interest paid, and F for the number of payments.

But what if you have 8K BASIC and therefore don't have the WHILE...WEND statement available? In that case we'd change the program to the following. Note that only a few of the lines are changed.

```
10 A = 25000 : B = 200 : C = .0075 : D = 0 : E = 0 : F = 0
20 PRINT "YEAR", "INTEREST PAID", "PRINCIPAL REMAINING"
30 FOR X = 1 TO 12
40 IF A<0 THEN G = 1 : GOTO 60
50 A = A + A*C - B : E = E + A*C : F = F + 1
60 NEXT X : IF G = 1 THEN 100
70 D = D + 1
80 PRINT 1982 + D,INT((E*100) + 5)/100,INT((A*100) + 5)/100
90 GOTO 30
100 PRINT 1982 + D + 1,"$";INT((E*100) + 5)/100,"$";
    INT((A*100) + 5)/100
110 PRINT F;"$200 PAYMENTS FOR A TOTAL OF $";F*B
```

Note that we didn't just jump out of the loop in line 40 by using

```
40 IF A<0 THEN 100
```

Another possibility would be to change line 40 to

```
40 IF A<0 THEN X = 13 : NEXT X : GOTO 100
```

and line 60 to

```
60 NEXT X
```

The idea is to complete all loops started one way or another. Not doing so can cause errors in later loops and crash the program. In this case the program was ending anyway and no harm would have been done, but it is best to be consistent. That's why it is best to use the WHILE loop in a case like this (if you have it in your BASIC).

THE READ STATEMENT

The READ statement (8K) is a very useful feature of BASIC. It is usually used with a FOR or WHILE loop, but not necessarily. It is used to assign values to a variable or variables. The values to be assigned are placed in a DATA block somewhere in the program. Here's a trivial example which calculates the average of a group of numbers found in a DATA line.

```
10 B = 0
20 FOR X = 1 TO 20
30 READ A : B = B + A
40 NEXT
50 PRINT "AVERAGE IS";B/20
60 DATA 8,10,15,7,5,6,3,9,1,2
70 DATA 3,9,7,25,10,6,4,1,3,7
```

You can also use a dummy value in the data line to tell BASIC the last data value has been reached.

```
10 B = 0 : C = 0
20 READ A : IF A = 999 THEN 50
30 B = B + A : C = C + 1
40 GOTO 20
50 PRINT "AVERAGE IS";B/C
60 DATA 8,10,15,7,5,6,3,9,1,2
70 DATA 3,9,7,25,10,6,4,1,3,7,999
```

Note also how the counter C was used to keep track of the number of data values.

DATA lines can be as long as is legal in that version of BASIC and can be anywhere in a program. They can be together or scattered around. The first READ statement always reads the first value in the first DATA statement, even if the DATA statement precedes it in the program (has a lower line number).

The RESTORE statement (8K) is used to begin reading the data again, starting at the first value in the first DATA line. To try it, just add line 115 to the previous program

```
115 RESTORE : GOTO 10
```

You'll have to use a control-C to exit the program after adding line 115.

If you try to READ more DATA values than are present in DATA statements, you will get an error message telling you so and the program will end. The message is "OUT OF DATA IN LINE XX", where XX is the line with the READ statement that caused the problem.

Finally, you cannot put any other statement (using the :) on a DATA line. Also, you can't put a REM on a DATA line. In other words, the only thing on a DATA line should be the data values.

You can put a line number after the RESTORE statement to start reading DATA at a specific line. Thus

```
10 B = 0 : INPUT "AVERAGE FIRST (1) or SECOND (2) GROUPS
   OF TEN VALUES";A
20 ON A GOTO 40,70
30 PRINT "USE 1 OR 2" : GOTO 10
40 FOR X = 1 TO 10
50 READ A : B = B + A
60 NEXT : GOTO 110
70 RESTORE 130
80 FOR X = 1 TO 10
90 READ A : B = B + A
100 NEXT
110 PRINT "THE AVERAGE IS";B/10
120 DATA 8,10,15,7,5,6,3,9,1,2
130 DATA 3,9,7,25,10,6,4,1,3,7
```

Note line 30 to catch any input over 2 from line 10.

Chapter Four

Arithmetic in BASIC

SINGLE PRECISION NUMBERS

As mentioned earlier, several types of numbers are used in
BASIC. All BASIC versions use single precision floating point.
That is, we have seven digits of precision and can display and
calculate with any number from 10E + 38 to 10E − 38. As you
will remember (I hope), the E represents scientific notation.
Let's take 123456789 as an example. It would be represented
in scientific notation as 1.234567E + 08; the E08 shows how
many decimal places follow the 1 (8 in the original number)
and only 6 digits of precision are displayed (seven are stored).
As another example, .00123456789 would be changed to
1.23457E − 03; the E − 03 shows the real position of the
decimal point, 3 to the left of that indicated, and the usual six
digits of precision are displayed and seven are stored. Thus
10E + 38 and 10E − 38 are extremely large and small numbers;
it is unlikely you will ever need larger or smaller ones.

INTEGER AND DOUBLE PRECISION NUMBERS

In EXTENDED BASIC we can also use integer and double
precision numbers. *Integers* are numbers without a decimal
point in the range from − 32768 to 32767. *Double precision*
numbers have the same range as single precision, but they
have up to 16 digits of precision (compared to 7 for single
precision). Numbers from .01 to 9999999999999999 are
displayed without reverting to the E format. (Incidentally, in

double precision D is used instead of E, thus 10D + 38 instead of 10E + 38.)

Single precision is assumed by BASIC unless you specify a variable as double precision or integer. A% would be an integer variable, A# would be a double precision variable, and A! or A would be a single precision variable. You can use A%, A, and A# in the same program and each can have a different value.

You should use integer variables (EXTENDED) whenever possible for a faster running program. BASIC can handle integers must faster than it can handle single or double precision numbers. For example, use integers to control in a FOR loop. Thus

```
10 FOR X = 1 TO 32000 : NEXT : PRINT "DONE"
```

took 65 seconds to run on my machine, while

```
10 FOR X% = 1 TO 32000 : NEXT : PRINT "DONE"
```

took 35 seconds.

Remember, integers are whole numbers so don't make a mistake like

```
FOR X% = 1 TO 100 STEP .5
```

The STEP .5 is illegal because the second value of X% is 1.5, which is not a legal integer value. Don't use integers in FOR loops where one of the limits or the STEP value might contain a decimal point or might exceed the − 32768 to 32767 limits of an integer.

OCTAL AND HEXADECIMAL NUMBERS

There are other forms of numbers you may wish to use in your programs: octal and hexadecimal (8K). It is assumed that you understand hex and octal notation, as a full explanation is beyond the scope and intent of this book. Many texts are available which explain these notations.

To assign an octal value use

```
10 A = &0247
```

or just

```
10 A = &247
```

This assigns variable A the decimal equivalent of octal 247.

```
10 A = &247
20 PRINT A
RUN
167
OK
```

The 167 is the decimal equivalent of octal 247. To designate a number as octal, use & or &O as a prefix. We handle hex numbers in a similar manner.

```
10 A = &H9A
20 PRINT A
RUN
154
OK
```

Again, 154 is the decimal equivalent of hex 9A. To designate a number as hexadecimal, use &H as a prefix.

To convert the other way, from decimal to hex or decimal to octal, we'd use HEX$(X) (EXTENDED) and OCT$(X) (EXTENDED), where X is the decimal number we wish to convert. A program to convert decimal numbers from 1 to 100 to hex and octal could be written as follows.

```
10 PRINT "DECIMAL","OCTAL","HEX"
20 FOR X% = 1 TO 100
30 PRINT X%,OCT$(X%),HEX$(X%)
40 NEXT
```

The HEX$(X) and OCT$(X) functions return the number in a string, not as a numeral you can calculate with. You have to add the &O or &H prefix to use them in a calculation. We'll see in a later chapter how this can be done under program control.

Note that hex and octal numbers are integers; they can't contain a decimal point. The HEX$(X) and OCT$(X) functions automatically round X off to an integer if it isn't one already.

PRECEDENCE OF OPERATIONS

Next we'll cover the operators used in BASIC programming. These are listed in order of *precedence*. Precedence is the order in which BASIC will evaluate expressions using these operators. This will become easier to understand as we go along.

( ) PARENTHESIS (8K): These are used to tell BASIC to evaluate the inside expression first, before using the other operators.

↑ EXPONENTIATION (8K): This is used to calculate the power of a number. Thus 3↑3 is the same as 3 cubed or 3 times 3 times 3. You cannot use a negative number following the ↑. Any number to the 0 power is equal to 1.

– NEGATION (8K): The unary minus operator. It denotes a negative number, not a subtraction.

∗,/ MULTIPLICATION and DIVISION (8K): Thus, 3∗3 means 3 times 3, 7/4 means 7 divided by 4.

\ INTEGER DIVISION (EXTENDED): This can be used for division of integers or integer variables. The / can also be used but the \ is faster.

MOD MODULUS ARITHMETIC (EXTENDED): For example, A MOD B gives the remainder after A is divided by B. Thus 6 MOD 4 would result in 2. The B variable cannot represent 0, as you cannot divide by 0. This could be written as

```
10 C = A
20 A = A – B : IF A = >B THEN 20
30 . . .
```

but of course the MOD operator is much faster.

+, – ADDITION AND SUBTRACTION (8K): This is normal arithmetic addition and subtraction. We've already seen many examples.

= EQUALS (8K): Self evident.

RELATIONAL OPERATORS:
<>Not equal (8K)
<Less than (8K)

>Greater than (8K)
< = Less than or equal to (8K)
= >Greater than or equal to (8K)
NOT Logical and bitwise negation (8K)
AND Logical and bitwise conjunction (8K)
OR Logical and bitwise disjunction (8K)
XOR Logical and bitwise exclusive OR (8K)
IMP Logical and bitwise implication (8K)
EQV Logical and bitwise equivalence (8K)
Now we'll explain how these work. Some are obvious, others not so obvious.

An example of using the parentheses could be illustrated by an attempt to multiply the sum of 2 plus 4 by 6. Writing

```
10 A = 2 + 4*6
```

would not work. You will note in the order of precedence that BASIC will perform the multiplication before the addition. So we'd get 26 as the value of A; that is, 4*6 = 24, 24 + 2 = 26. To get the result we wish, we'd write

```
10 A = (2 + 4)*6
```

Since BASIC does the calculation in parentheses before the multiplication, A would be given the value of 36 (2 + 4 = 6, 6*6 = 36). To cause BASIC to do calculations out of the usual order of precedence, use the parentheses. Also, when in doubt, use the parentheses.

Negation just means a negative number, - 3, - 2.5, etc.

Integer division automatically rounds the dividend and the divisor to integers, and rounds the quotient to an integer, if necessary. The dividend and divisor must be in the integer range, - 32768 to 32767. As noted earlier, we could also use the regular division sign (/) but BASIC performs the operation more quickly when the integer division sign (\) is used. Of course, the regular division sign does not convert any of the values to integer.

To explain the relational operators we'll use truth tables. Truth tables show the results of all possible combinations of the two variables for the relational operator used.

NOT

X	NOT X
0	1
1	0

AND

X	Y	X AND Y
0	0	0
0	1	0
1	0	0
1	1	1

OR

X	Y	X OR Y
0	0	0
0	1	1
1	0	1
1	1	1

XOR

X	Y	X XOR Y
0	0	0
0	1	1
1	0	1
1	1	0

IMP

X	Y	X IMP Y
0	0	1
0	1	1
1	0	0
1	1	1

EQV

X	Y	X EQV Y
0	0	1
0	1	0
1	0	0
1	1	1

We can use these logical expressions in IF statements. In fact, this is where they are usually found.

```
10 IF X = 4 AND Y = 3 THEN Z = 7
20 IF X = 4 OR Y = 3 THEN Z = 7
30 IF A = NOT B THEN Z = 7
```

The last one means if $A = 1$ and $B = -1$ then $Z = 7$ (NOT $-1 = 0$). We will see how such expressions can be used in a moment.

Next we see the logical assignment statement.

```
40 A = B<C
```

If the statement "B<C" is true, A is assigned the value of -1, representing TRUE. If the statement is false, A is assigned the value 0, representing FALSE. For example, if $B = 6$ and $C = 12$, the relation is TRUE and A is assigned the value -1. If $B = 12$ and $C = 6$, the relation is FALSE and A is assigned the value 0.

Here's another way we can use relational operators. Let's suppose we want to set the variable K to a value of 6 if A = >4, 5 if A = >3, 4 if A = >2, 3 if A = >1, and 2 if A is less than 1. (The = > means equal to or greater than.) We would write

10 K = 2 − ((A = >4) + (A = >3) + (A = >2) + (A = >1))

Then if A = 3 then A = >4 would be 0 (FALSE), A = >3 would be − 1 (TRUE), A = >2 would be − 1 (TRUE), and A = >1 would be − 1 (TRUE). Adding everything we'd have 2 − ((0) + (− 1) + (− 1)), or 2 − (− 3), or 5. Thus, K would be 5. Another longer and slower way to write this would be

```
10 IF A=>1 THEN K=1
20 IF A=>2 THEN K=2
30 IF A=>3 THEN K=3
40 IF A=>4 THEN K=4
50 K=K+2
```

Keep that faster way in mind; when you find a place for it in a program it can save writing a lot of program lines. Note the order of statements in the latter program. If we had written

```
10 IF A=>4 THEN K=4
20 IF A=>3 THEN K=3
30 IF A=>2 THEN K=2
40 IF A=>1 THEN K=1
50 K=K+2
```

then the program would not work correctly. If A = 3 then K would equal 3 after line 50. Not the right answer. This type of program sequence occurs quite frequently. The IF statements must be placed in the correct order to get the right results. To make the last program run correctly we could add : GOTO 50 to lines 10 through 30.

The relational operators can also be used for bit by bit (binary) comparisons. Here are a few numbers and their binary equivalents.

0 = 0000		
1 = 0001	4 = 0100	7 = 0111
2 = 0010	5 = 0101	8 = 1000
3 = 0011	6 = 0110	9 = 1001

So 6 OR 7 would result in a value of 7; that is, 6 = 0110 and 7 = 0111. ORing the bits:

```
0110
0111 OR
0111 RESULT
```

Also, 2 AND 6 = 2:

```
0010
0110 AND
0010 RESULT
```

Binary comparisons like this can be used to test data input from a computer port while waiting for a certain condition to occur. See the WAIT and INP commands for examples.

At first, you'll use the AND and OR relational operators most often. Once you have more programming experience, you'll find a number of uses for the others described in this chapter.

Here are a few random lines showing examples of the use of relational operators.

```
10 IF A>B OR C<D THEN 1100
20 IF A = >D AND C = 7 THEN GOSUB 70
30 IF A = 7 AND (B = 7 OR C = 8) THEN D = 9
40 IF A<>10 THEN A = 1
50 IF C<>4 OR (B = C AND D = X) THEN 1000
```

Now for an example program using some of these operators just discussed. We'll design a perpetual calendar starting at January 1, 1800. It would print out the day of the week for any date given. Remember, a year divisible by 4 is a leap year, giving February 29 days. If a year is evenly divisible by 100, it also has to be evenly divisible by 400 to be a leap year. Thus, 1700, 1800, and 1900 are not leap years, but 2000 is.

We'll assign each day of the week a number (Sunday = 0, Monday = 1, Tuesday = 2, etc.) and convert it to the day of the week when we print it out. We have to have a starting day for January 1, 1800. A little research shows it was a Wednesday, or a 3 in our assignment scheme. So here's one way we could write the program.

```
20 PRINT "PLEASE ENTER THE DATE FOR WHICH YOU WISH
   TO"
30 PRINT "KNOW THE DAY OF THE WEEK. ENTER"
40 PRINT "THE MONTH FIRST (JAN = 1, FEB = 2, ETC.),"
50 PRINT "THEN A COMMA, THEN THE DAY, THEN "
60 PRINT "ANOTHER COMMA, FOLLOWED BY THE YEAR"
70 PRINT "(1800 to 2000) AND THEN A CARRIAGE RETURN."
80 D = 3 : INPUT "DATE";A,B,C
90 IF C<1800 THEN PRINT "THE YEAR MUST BE LATER THAN
   1800" : GOTO 80
95 IF C>2000 THEN PRINT "LESS THAN YEAR 2000,
   PLEASE" : GOTO 80
100 IF A>12 THEN 600 REM INVALID DATA
110 IF B>31 THEN 600
120 IF A = 4 OR A = 6 OR A = 9 OR A = 11 AND B>30 THEN 600
130 IF C/4<>INT(C/4) AND A = 2 AND B>28 THEN 600
140 IF C/100 = INT(C/100) AND A = 2 AND B>28 THEN 600
150 C = C - 1800 REM YEARS TO DATE
160 E = INT(C/4) REM ADD LEAP YEARS
170 E = E - INT(C/100) - 1 REM SUBTRACT YEARS DIVISIBLE
   BY 100
175 IF A<3 AND B<29 AND INT(C/4) = C/4 THEN E = E - 1
180 F = C + E : REM DAYS TO YEAR INPUT
190 ON A GOSUB 300,310,320,330,340,350,360,370,380,390,
   400,410
200 F = F + G + B
210 D = D + F
215 D = D - 7 : IF D>6 THEN 215 REM IF YOU HAVE THE
   COMMAND USE D = D MOD 7 AS LINE 215
220 ON D + 1 GOTO 500,510,520,530,540,550,560
299 REM NUMBER OF DAYS IN YEAR SO FAR
300 G = 0 : RETURN
310 G = 31 : RETURN
320 G = 59 : RETURN
330 G = 90 : RETURN
340 G = 120 : RETURN
350 G = 151 : RETURN
360 G = 181 : RETURN
370 G = 212 : RETURN
390 G = 243 : RETURN
400 G = 304 : RETURN
410 G = 334 : RETURN
```

```
499 REM DAY OF WEEK
500 PRINT "SUNDAY" : GOTO 570
510 PRINT "MONDAY" : GOTO 570
520 PRINT "TUESDAY" : GOTO 570
530 PRINT "WEDNESDAY" : GOTO 570
540 PRINT "THURSDAY" : GOTO 570
550 PRINT "FRIDAY" : GOTO 570
560 PRINT "SATURDAY" : GOTO 570
570 INPUT "ANOTHER";A$
580 IF A$ = "YES" THEN 80
590 END
600 PRINT "NOT A VALID DATE, TRY AGAIN." : GOTO 80
```

As written, the program will only work properly for dates up to 12/31/1999. Why? Hint, see line 170 (of course, also line 95!). How could you modify it to work for any date in the future? The program will only work for dates after 1/1/1800. How could you modify it to work for earlier dates? What is the earliest date you could set the program for? (Remember the calendar reform.)

Now see if you can write a program to calculate how long it would take to double a given amount of money in a savings account at 5% interest, compounded monthly. Would the initial amount of money in the account have any effect on the time? How much difference would it make if the interest were compounded daily? Try other interest rates. Try writing the program so the interest rate, the frequency of compounding the interest, the starting date, and the amount of money you start with are all variables set by answering questions asked by the program. The program should print out the date at which the account reaches or exceeds double the starting amount.

INTRINSIC FUNCTIONS

Intrinsic functions perform operations that would normally require a subroutine if they were not available. In all cases to follow, the X in parentheses is the variable, constant, or expression operated on. The functions are listed in alphabetical order.

ABS(X) (8K): This returns the absolute value of the number. ABS(4) = 4 and ABS(– 4) = 4. ABS is usually used to convert a possibly negative number to a positive number for a program operation or for a printout. For example, a charge account customer might make too large a payment, giving a negative amount owed. In the statement, this might be converted to a positive number preceded or followed by the word CREDIT.

ATN(X) (8K): This returns the arctangent of X. The result is given in radians in the range $-\pi/2$ to $\pi/2$. The result is returned in single precision. To get the answer in degrees, multiply the radian result by 57.2958. For example, A = ATN(X)*57.2958: A would now be in degrees.

CINT(X), CSNG(X), CDBL(X) (EXTENDED): This converts X respectively to an integer, single precision, or double precision. So:

```
A% = CINT(X)
```

X must be in the range -32768 to 32767. Note this is not the same as INT(X), which will operate on any single precision number.

```
A = CSNG(X)
```

could be used to convert a double precision number to single precision if X is double precision. Remember, X can also be a constant or expression.

```
A# = CDBL(X)
```

could be used to convert a single precision number to double precision. Watch out for this one if you are interested in very accurate results. For example:

```
10 A = 2.04
20 B# = CDBL(A)
30 PRINT A,B#
RUN
2.04  2.039999961853027
```

To avoid problems like this, stick to either single or double precision and don't mix them. Also, remember these intrinsic functions, with the exception of CDBL(X) and CINT(X), return single precision results. Converting them to double precision will not make them more accurate.

COS(X) (8K): This returns the cosine of X, where X is in radians. To use an X expressed in degrees instead of radians, write as COS(X/57.2958).

EXP(X) (8K): This returns e to the power X. X must be $\leq = 87.3364$. The value of e is 2.71828; it is the base for *natural logarithms*, as opposed to logarithms based on 10 (also known as *common logarithms*).

FIX(X) (EXTENDED): This is equivalent to the expression SGN(X)*INT(ABS(X)). The difference between INT(X) and FIX(X) is shown in the following program.

```
10 PRINT FIX(4.1)
20 PRINT INT(4.1)
30 PRINT FIX( - 4.1)
40 PRINT INT( - 4.1)
RUN
4       4       -4       -5
```

Unlike INT(X), FIX(X) does not return the next lower integer when X is negative. X can be any single precision number.

INT(X) (8K): This was explained earlier. It returns the next lower integer of a number X. The value of X can be any single precision number.

LOG(X) (8K): This returns the natural log (log to base e or base 2.71828) of X. To convert to common log or log base 10, use

```
A = LOG(X)*.4343
```

X must be greater than 0.

RND(X) (8K): This returns a random number between 0 and 1. The same sequence of random numbers is generated each time the program is run unless the random number generator is reseeded. To reseed the generator, use the command RANDOMIZE in the program before the first RND statement. However, X<0 always restarts the same sequence for any given X.

If the X is omitted or X>0, then the next random number in the sequence is generated. If X = 0 then the last random number is repeated.

To get an integer random number between 1 and X, use

```
A = INT(RND*X + 1)
```

To get a decimal random number between 0 and X, use

```
A = RND*X
```

SGN(X) (8K): This returns – 1 if X<0, 0 if X = 0, and + 1 if X>0. One common use for SGN(X) is to branch to a different program line based on whether the value of X is negative, zero, or positive. Thus in the example,

```
10 ON SGN(X) + 2 GOTO 100,200,300
```

If X is negative the program will branch to line 100, if X is positive the program will branch to line 300, and if X is zero the program will branch to line 200. Something like this might be used in a charge account program to treat the balance differently depending on whether there was still an account balance owed, the account was paid in full, or the account was overpaid (credit).

SIN(X) (8K): This returns the sine of X, where X is in radians. See COS(X) for degree conversion.

SQR(X) (8K): This returns the square root of the value X. X must be = >0.

TAN(X) (8K): This returns the tangent of X, where X is in radians. See COS(X) for degree conversion.

The above functions, from ABS(X) on, all give answers in single precision. with the exception of CDBL(X) and CINT(X).

Let's try one short program illustrating the use of some of these functions.

```
10 PRINT "THIS PROGRAM DISPLAYS A LIST"
20 PRINT "OF THE SINES OF ANGLES BETWEEN 0"
30 PRINT "AND 360."
40 PRINT "DEGREES","SINE"
```

```
50 FOR X% = 1 TO 360
60 PRINT X%,SIN(X%/57.2958)
70 NEXT
```

How would you convert this program to print the sine, cosine, and tangent of the angles? How would you convert it to print out the values for every tenth of a degree? How could you compute the cotangent? The secant? The cosecant?

USER DEFINED FUNCTIONS

DEF FN(X) (8K): While DEF is not an intrinsic function, I believe you will find it most useful. This function is used to provide an easy way to use a long expression more than once without writing it out each time. As you will see, it serves a different purpose than a subroutine. Here's an example.

```
10 DEF FNA(V) = (SIN(V)*57.2958)*.51/180
20 Z = FNA(30)
```

As you can see, once we define (DEF) the long formula in line 10, (SIN(V)*57.2958)*.51/180, we can use it by writing an expression like that in line 20. The V in parentheses in line 10 is the variable which is assigned a value each time the function is used. So, in this case, we used the constant 30 in line 20 to replace the V in the formula in line 10.

Each DEF expression must be named FN followed by a legal variable name. In the case above, we used A, but any variable name could have been used. You can use several variables (EXTENDED) in parentheses. Thus:

```
10 DEF FNSUM(A,B,C) = A + B + C
20 INPUT "VALUE #1";D
30 INPUT "VALUE #2";E
40 INPUT "VALUE #3";F
50 PRINT FNSUM(D,E,F)
```

Note that the variables used in line 10 are different than the variables used in line 50. This is permissible and usually done. Another example is a DEF line used to generate random numbers in any range selected.

```
10 RANDOMIZE : DEF FNR(A) = INT(RND*A + 1)
20 R = FNR(10)
```

Whatever number (or variable) is used in line 20 after the FNR determines the maximum value of the returned random number. Note that so far we have only used numeric variables. Those are the only ones permitted in 8K BASIC. In the EXTENDED or DISK versions of BASIC, string variables can be used too.

```
10 DEF FNA$(B$,V) = RIGHT$(B$,V)
```

The DEF statement must appear in the program prior to the first FN statement that references that function. Note that FN is illegal as a variable name except as described above.

You will save programming time and memory if you use the DEF function whenever possible. It will pay you to go back over a long program after you've finished it and replace long expressions used several times in the program with DEF statements wherever possible.

To get a little practice using DEF, try writing a program that will shoot craps with you. For the uninitiated, this program requires two dice. If the first throw by the player is a 7 or 11 the player wins; if a 2, 3, or 12 the player loses. If any other number (the player rolls until he gets that number (his point) or rolls a 7 and loses. The player and the computer should take turns. The game is slightly against the dice roller (shooter). Use random numbers from 1 to 6 for each die. The player and the computer should start out with a stake and bet consistently. The first to go broke loses. Be sure to use DEF statements wherever possible.

Here's another program that might be more interesting. Let's say there is a supermarket game that gives you one of 50 different numbered cards (from 1 to 50) for each purchase. Using random numbers, see how many purchases would be required to get a full set of numbers. Assume the odds are equal for getting any number. Run the program, say 100 times, and get an average of the number of purchases required. You might be surprised at the answer.

Chapter Five

Strings

We mentioned string variables a few times in earlier chapters. We use string variables to store alphanumeric information (letters, punctuation, and numerals). Thus we could use

```
A$ = "$100"
A$ = "234"
A$ = "FRANK"
A$ = "FUZZY WUZZY WAS A BEAR. FUZZY WUZZY HAD NO
     HAIR. FUZZY WUZZY WASN'T VERY FUZZY WAS HE?"
```

We also mentioned that any spaces within quotation marks are retained. Also, you cannot put quotation marks within quotation marks. Thus

```
A$ = "MICHAEL "MIKE" JONES"
```

is illegal. A string can consist of 0 to 255 characters. The string " " is a null string, of 0 length.

Strings can be used with the relational operators =, <, >, <=, and =>. For example:

```
10 IF A$ = "JOHN" AND B$ = "JONES" THEN 100
```

or

```
10 IF A$>B$ THEN 250
```

When evaluating relations involving strings comparisons of the ASCII values of the characters in the string are used. The ASCII values of all the alphanumerics are given in appendix A. During expression evalution, the ASCII values of the characters are compared and the lower code is considered less in the comparison. Also, if the strings are not the same length, the shorter string is considered the lesser. One use of this would be to put words in alphabetical order.

We can also use the + sign to put words together (concatenation).

```
10 A$ = "JOHN" : B$ = "JONES" : C$ = " JONES" : D$ = " "
20 E$ = A$ + B$ : F$ = A$ + C$ : G$ = A$ + D$ + B$
30 PRINT E$,F$,G$
RUN
JOHNJONES      JOHN JONES      JOHN JONES
OK
```

Note that we must supply the separating space (if required) when concatenating strings. Also, you can only use the + sign; the −, /, *, etc. will not work. Note also

```
10 A$ = "FRANK" : B$ = "FRANK "
20 IF A$ = B$ THEN PRINT "EQUAL" ELSE PRINT "NOT EQUAL"
30 RUN
NOT EQUAL
OK
```

String B$ was longer so it was considered greater in value. The difference in length was caused by the trailing space in B$. Watch out for this. If you don't get string equality when you expect it, look for leading or trailing spaces in one of the strings. You are likely to have this problem when using strings in random disk files. One way to check is to cause the string to be printed within bracketing characters to make the space(s) visible. For example, using the previous contents of A$ and B$

```
PRINT "X";A$;"X","X";B$;"X"
XFRANKX      XFRANK X
```

You could also use the LEN( ) command, to be described later in this chapter.

INTRINSIC FUNCTIONS

As we noted earlier, you can use string variables in INPUT, DEF, etc. The following are some very useful intrinsic functions for use with strings.

ASC(X$) (8K): This returns the ASCII value of the first character in string X$. See Appendix A for the values returned. If X$ is a null string you will get an error.

```
PRINT ASC("A")
65
```

or

```
A$ = "A" : PRINT ASC(A$)
65
```

CHR$(X) (8K): This returns the string representation of the ASCII value X. It is frequently used to send a special character to the terminal, such as a carriage return, CHR$(13); ring the bell, CHR$(7); etc. The command has many other uses when you wish to convert a numeric value to its ASCII representation. For example:

```
10 RANDOMIZE
20 R = INT(RND(1)*26 + 1)
30 R$ = CHR$(64 + R) : PRINT R$ : GOTO 10
```

You can also print CHR$( ) directly. For example,

```
10 PRINT CHR$(10)
```

will send a line feed to the terminal.

One interesting use of CHR$( ) and ASC( ) is to store a value between 0 and 255 in a single byte, perhaps to POKE into a single memory location or to use in disk files to save space. A single precision number requires four bytes of space, an integer two bytes.

HEX$(X) (EXTENDED): This function will return a string representation of the hexadecimal value of the value represented by X$. Thus:

```
10 A$ = HEX$(75)
20 D = VAL("&H" + A$)
30 PRINT A$,D
RUN
4B        75
```

Note that the result of HEX$( ) is a string, not a number. In
line 20 we had to add "&H" to A$ and use the function VAL( )
to get back to the original number. (See the section on hexadecimal numbers.) VAL( ) will be described a little later in
this chapter.

INKEY$ (8K): If you wish to get input from the terminal
one character at a time, use this function. It is also useful
when you do not wish to require the operator to enter the CR
after his or her input. This requires that you anticipate exactly
how many characters will be used. For example:

```
10 GOSUB 50 : B = A : GOSUB 50 : PRINT "SUM = ";A + B : END
50 PRINT "ENTER SINGLE DIGIT NUMBER" : Z$ = " "
60 Z$ = INKEY$ : IF Z$ = " " THEN 60
70 IF Z$<"0" OR Z$>"9" THEN 60
80 A = VAL(Z$) : RETURN
```

In this little program line 60 uses the INKEY$ command. Note
how the variable Z$ is tested until it picks up a keyboard
character via INKEY$. In line 50 Z$ is set to a null string so
the test in line 60 will work properly. You must use a test such
as shown in line 60 to keep the INKEY$ in a loop until a key is
pressed on the terminal. You could also use

```
60 Z$ = INKEY$ : IF LEN(Z$) = 0 THEN 60
```

since a null string has a length of 0. See LEN( ) command later
in this chapter. Another example:

```
10 PRINT "TOTALS NOW (Y OR N)? "; : A$ = " "
20 A$ = INKEY$ : IF A$ = " " THEN 20
30 PRINT A$
40 IF A$ = "Y" THEN 1000
50 IF A$ = "N" THEN 2000
60 PRINT "USE Y OR N" : GOTO 10
```

You will note that the characters are not echoed on the terminal when using INKEY$; this is the reason for line 30.

You can also use INKEY$ to replace the LINE INPUT statement in 8K BASIC. Thus,

```
10 LINE INPUT "NAME? "; N$
20 . . .
```

can be replaced with

```
10 N$ = " " : A$ = " "
20 PRINT "NAME? ";
30 A$ = INKEY$ : IF A$ = " " THEN 30
40 IF A$ = CHR$(13) THEN PRINT : GOTO 60
50 N$ = N$ + A$ : PRINT A$; : A$ = " " : GOTO 30
```

INSTR(I,X$,Y$) (EXTENDED): This function is used to return the position of the character (or string) Y$ in X$. Optional variable I sets the point where the search is to begin. If I is not provided, it is defaulted to 1. If I is greater than the length of X$, if X$ is a null string, or if Y$ cannot be found, then a 0 is returned. If Y$ is null, then I or a 1 is returned. If I is 0, you will get an error.

```
10 A$ = "MICROSOFT"
20 B$ = "O" : C$ = "Z"
30 PRINT INSTR(A$,B$),INSTR(6,A$,B$),INSTR(A$,C$)
RUN
 5       7       0
OK
```

Variable B$ can be more than one character in length.

LEFT$(A$,X) (8K): This is a very useful function. It will select a group of characters from the left end of a string where A$ is the string and X is the number of characters. If X is greater than the length of A$, the contents of A$ are returned. If X is 0, then a null string is returned. Thus:

```
10 A$ = "MICROSOFT"
20 B$ = LEFT$(A$,5)
30 PRINT B$
```

```
RUN
MICRO
OK
```

LEN(X$) (8K): This function is used to find out how many characters there are in a string, where X$ is the string in question. If X$ is a null string, a 0 is returned. For example:

```
10 INPUT "ENTER A STRING";A$
20 PRINT A$;" IS";LEN(A$);"CHARACTERS LONG"
30 PRINT "ANOTHER (Y OR N)? ";
40 Z$ = " "
50 Z$ = INKEY$ : IF LEN(Z$) = 0 THEN 50
60 PRINT Z$
70 IF Z$ = "Y" THEN 10
80 IF Z$ = "N" THEN END
90 PRINT "USE Y OR N" : GOTO 30
```

This example demonstrates several uses for LEN( ).

MID$(X$,I,J) (8K): This function is a little like LEFT$( ), but returns characters from anywhere in a string. In use it returns a string J characters long, starting at the I*th* character, from string X$. If J is not given, or if there are fewer than J characters to the right of the I*th* character, then the I*th* characters and all characters to its right are returned.

```
10 A$ = "MY CAT HAS FLEAS"
20 PRINT MID$(A$,4,3),MID$(A$,12)
RUN
CAT        FLEAS
OK
```

OCT$(X) (EXTENDED): This function is used to return a string representing the value of X in octal format.

```
10 A$ = OCT$(8)
20 PRINT A$,VAL("&0" + A$)
RUN
10        8
OK
```

See HEX$( ) for a similar function.

RIGHT$(A$,X) (8K): This function is like LEFT$( ), but it returns X characters from the right end of the string contained in variable A$. If X is equal to or greater than the length of A$, then A$ is returned. If X = 0 then a null string is returned.

```
10 A$ = "MICROSOFT"
20 FOR X = 1 TO LEN(A$)
30 B$ = RIGHT$(A$,X)
40 PRINT B$
50 NEXT
RUN
T
FT
OFT
SOFT
OSOFT
ROSOFT
CROSOFT
ICROSOFT
MICROSOFT
OK
```

SPACE$(X) (EXTENDED): This function returns a string of spaces of length X. The expression X must not exceed 255.

```
10 FOR X = 0 TO 5
20 A$ = "X";SPACE$(X);"X" : PRINT A$
30 NEXT
RUN
XX
X X
X  X
X   X
X    X
X     X
OK
```

SPC(X) (8K): Like SPACE$(X), this function returns a string of 0 to 255 spaces. However, while SPACE$(X) may be assigned to a string variable (A$ = SPACE$(15), for example), SPC(X) must be used directly in a PRINT or LPRINT statement. Thus:

```
10 FOR X = 0 TO 5
20 PRINT "X";SPC(X);"X"
30 NEXT
```

The program output is the same as the previous example.

STR$(X) (8K): This is a very useful function that converts a number to its string representation. For example,

```
10 S$ = STR$(40)
```

would result in S$ = 40. Note that 40 is now a string, not a number; it can no longer be used in a calculation. However, it can be treated as a string and used with any string functions.

```
10 INPUT "MONTH (JAN = 1, ETC)";M
20 INPUT "DAY";D
30 INPUT "YEAR (1980)";Y
40 IF M<10 THEN M$ = "0" + RIGHT$(STR$(M),1) : GOTO 60
50 M$ = RIGHT$(STR$(M),2)
60 IF D<10 THEN D$ = "0" + RIGHT$(STR$(D),1) : GOTO 80
70 D$ = RIGHT$(STR$(D),2)
80 Y$ = RIGHT$(STR$(Y),2)
90 PRINT "DATE IS ";M$ + "/" + "D$" + "/" + Y$
RUN
MONTH (JAN = 1, ETC.)? 6
DAY? 6
YEAR (1980)? 1981
DATE IS 06/06/81
OK
```

STRING$(X,Y) (EXTENDED): This returns a string of length X consisting of characters whose ASCII value is Y. Thus:

```
10 A$ = STRING$(6,42) : B$ = " SUMMARY " : PRINT A$;B$;A$
RUN
***** SUMMARY *****
OK
```

Think of this function whenever you repeatedly use a string of identical characters in a program.

TAB(X) (8K): Here is a function you will use frequently. It spaces to the X*th* position on a line. If the current position on the line exceeds the value X, then TAB goes to the X*th* position on the next line. X must be in the range 1 to 255, and it can be a constant, expression, or variable.

```
10 PRINT "NAME" TAB(25) "PHONE" : PRINT
20 READ A$,B$
30 PRINT A$ TAB(25) B$
40 DATA CHARLIE, 234-5678
RUN
NAME          PHONE
CHARLIE       234-5678
OK
```

VAL(X$) (8K): This function is the opposite of STR$(X). VAL(X$) prints out the value of a string of digits. It also removes any spaces, TABs, etc., from the string X$. Thus:

```
10 A$ = "    −56"
20 PRINT VAL(A$)
RUN
−56
OK
```

The result of VAL is a number, not a string, and can be used in calculations.

Here's a program that uses several of the functions we've discussed in this chapter. It converts a decimal number to a Roman numeral.

```
10 INPUT "NUMBER, NOT OVER 1999";A : X = 0
20 IF A>1999 OR A<0 THEN 10
30 A$ = STR$(A) : B$ = " " : A$ = RIGHT$(A$,LEN(A$) − 1)
40 FOR Y = LEN(A$) TO 1 STEP − 1 : X = X + 1
50 GOSUB 100
60 B$ = C$ + B$
70 NEXT
80 PRINT "THE ANSWER IS ";B$ : INPUT "ANOTHER (Y/N)";
   A$ : IF A$ = "Y" THEN 10
90 END
```

```
100 D$ = MID$(A$,X,1)
110 ON Y GOSUB 300,310,320,330
120 ON VAL(D$) + 1 GOTO 130,140,150,160,170,180,190,200,
    210,220
130 C$ = " " : RETURN
140 C$ = S$ : RETURN
150 C$ = S$ + S$ : RETURN
160 C$ = S$ + S$ + S$ : RETURN
170 C$ = S$ + L$ : RETURN
180 C$ = L$ : RETURN
190 C$ = L$ + S$ : RETURN
200 C$ = L$ + S$ + S$ : RETURN
210 C$ = L$ + S$ + S$ + S$ : RETURN
220 C$ = S$ + V$
300 S$ = "I" : L$ = "V" : V$ = "X" : RETURN
310 S$ = "X" : L$ = "L" : V$ = "M" : RETURN
320 S$ = "C" : L$ = "D" : V$ = "M" : RETURN
330 S$ = "M" : RETURN
```

The third statement in line 30 is used to remove the leading space in string A. How would you like to write a program to convert from Roman numerals to decimal? How about a program to add (or subtract) two Roman numerals by converting them to decimal, doing the calculation, then converting the answer back to Roman numerals? If you really feel ambitious, see if you can write a program to directly add (or subtract) in Roman numerals. Pity those poor Romans!

Here's another program. This one prints out a list of numbers from a DATA block with an added $.

```
10 PRINT "DATE", "RECEIPTS"
20 FOR X = 1 TO 30
30 READ A
40 PRINT X,"$";A
50 NEXT : END
70 DATA 97.42,39.17,1040.17,996.42,456
80 DATA 9.16,27.12,1047.14,127.72,14.17
90 DATA 12,4.20,.44,1067.42,943.10
100 DATA .14,1067,94.23,18.12,27.10
110 DATA 1062.12,148,9,4.12,9.14
```

This program will print a nice column of figures, but some will have decimal points and others won't, and the ones with decimal points don't line up very well. Your mission, should you accept it, is to write a program that adds the decimal point and two zeros to even dollar figures, and prints the receipts with all the decimal points in a nice orderly column. Also, get rid of the space between the $ and the number, or have the dollar signs all print in one column. No fair using the PRINT USING statement described next.

PRINT USING (EXTENDED): This statement is used to format printout. It is very useful for reports, business programs, and even games. This statement lets you determine where the decimal point should appear, add a $ to a figure, etc. It works with both strings and numbers. Here's an example.

```
10 A = 453.2
20 PRINT USING "###.##";A
RUN
453.20
OK
```

As you can see, A is printed as 453.20. The 0 was added after the 2 because we requested two digits after the decimal point (.##) in the pattern provided. The #'s in the pattern supplied after PRINT USING determine the format of the number. Thus, in the pattern in the example we want up to three digits before the decimal point, and two after the decimal point. If the number supplied has less than two digits after the decimal point, the empty space will be filled with a zero, as in the example. If the number has more than two digits, it will be rounded off to two digits after the decimal point.

Of course the pattern can be whatever we wish, with as many digits before and after the decimal point as desired. In the example the pattern was supplied in quotes after the PRINT USING. We could also store the pattern in a string variable if it is to be used in more than one statement. Thus:

```
10 A$ = "###.##"
20 A = 453.2
```

```
30 PRINT USING A$;A
RUN
453.20
OK
```

Another example:

```
10 READ A
20 IF A = 999 THEN 40
30 PRINT A : GOTO 10
40 PRINT : RESTORE
50 READ A
60 IF A = 999 THEN END
70 PRINT USING " # # # # . # # ";A : GOTO 50
90 DATA 1,50,100.1,1000,12.346,1024.99,1.1
100 DATA 250,999
RUN
1
50
100.1
1000
12.346
1024.99
1.1
250

   1.00
  50.00
 100.10
1000.00
  12.35
1024.99
   1.10
 250.00
```

Note how neat the second row of figures looks; all the decimal points are in a vertical line and all the rightmost digits are neatly lined up. You can see how much nicer this would look in a report. If the number supplied was too long to fit into the pattern (####.##), let's say it was 10423.64, it would be displayed as %10423.64, the % pointing out that the number was too long for the pattern. Note also how the 12.346 was rounded off to 12.35. Numbers with less than the desired number of digits in front of the decimal point are filled out with spaces as shown in the example. PRINT USING can only be used for numbers with up to 24 digits.

The decimal point can be placed anywhere in the format field (pattern); thus #.###, ###.#, .##, etc. A single comma placed before the decimal point will cause a comma to be placed every three digits in front of the decimal point when the number is output.

```
10 A$ = "#########,.##"
20 FOR X = 1 TO 5
30 READ A
40 PRINT USING A$;A
50 NEXT
DATA 1234.56,123456,1234567,12345,1234567899
RUN
          1,234.56
        123,456.00
      1,234,567.00
         12,345.00
%1,234,567,899.00
OK
```

There are many other ways to use PRINT USING. Here are some examples of formats, numbers, and the resulting output.

FORMAT	NUMBER	RESULT
##	12	12
###	12	12
#####,.##	1200	1,200.00
##.##	12	12.00
###,.	12	12.
#.###	.02	0.020
##.#	2.36	2.4
#.##	−12	% −12.00
###	−12	−12
###−	−12	12−
+###	12	+12
−###	−12	−12
−###	12	12
##	12.36	12

```
.###          .9999          %1.000
+###          -12            -12
```

If two asterisks are placed before the number, the leading spaces in the number will be filled with asterisks (*).

```
**####        12             ****12
**#.#         127            127.0
```

If the double dollar sign $$ is placed before the pattern, a dollar sign will be placed immediately before the first digit of the number.

```
$$###.##      12             $12.00
```

A combination of these last two features is handy for check printing.

```
**$#####.##   12.34          *****$12.34
**$#####.##   1234           ***$1234.00
```

If four carats or up arrows (↑↑↑↑) are placed after the definition field, the number will be printed in exponential format.

```
##↑↑↑↑         -12           -1.2E+01
##↑↑↑↑         12            1.2E+01
.####↑↑↑↑ -    12            .1200E+02
+.##↑↑↑↑       -12.345       -.12E+02
+.##↑↑↑↑       12.345        +.12E+02
```

Finally, PRINT USING works on strings, too. The ! leaves room for one character, the double backslash leaves room for each space between the slashes +2. Trailing spaces will be used to fill if the string doesn't fill the area.

```
\  \          ABCD           ABCD
\  \          ABCDE          ABCD
\ \           ABC            ABC
!             ABC            A
\\            ABCD           AB
```

If you use an &, the string will be repeated exactly as input.

```
&          ABC            ABC
&          ABCDEFG        ABCDEFG
```

Here's an example using strings and numbers.

```
10 READ A$,A
20 IF A$ = "END" THEN END
30 PRINT USING " \        \ ARE NOW $####.##";A$,A
40 GOTO 10
50 DATA STOCKS,1253.62,BONDS,4327,UTILITIES,317.2
60 DATA END,0
RUN
STOCKS   ARE NOW $1253.62
BONDS    ARE NOW $4327.00
UTILITIES ARE NOW  $317.20
```

You can see that strings can be added to a PRINT USING line (STOCKS, BONDS, etc.), or that they can be part of the line (the ARE NOW). This feature can be used to line up the data very nicely in whatever format you desire. Note that the format pattern must be in quotation marks or stored in a string variable. You might remember that strings can be built up in a program using concatenation, thus allowing a PRINT USING pattern to be dynamically created by a program.

Be sure you use a string variable, expression, or constant when PRINT USING expects a string, and a numeric variable, constant, or expression when a number is expected. The examples all used READ to get input for the PRINT USING statements. Of course this is not necessary; the data can be acquired with INPUT statements, calculated or created by the program, or computed using any other valid method of getting data into a variable. As mentioned earlier, the data can also be a constant placed directly in the string (the ARE NOW used in the last program).

Try writing some programs to test your understanding of PRINT USING. That's the best way to learn.

Chapter Six

Editing

An at sign (@) following an input (program INPUT, LINE INPUT statement, or typing in a program line) lets you repeat the line. Typing the left (back) arrow, delete key, or rubout key (depending on the terminal) lets you reenter the last character. This is called line editing. In EXTENDED BASIC you can also recall a program line and edit it without retyping the whole line. This is called character editing.

To get the line you wish to edit, enter EDIT and the line number. Enter

```
EDIT 100
```

to get line 100. BASIC will reply by typing 100 on the next line, then stopping. You can now edit the line. To edit a line you just entered or just finished editing, type EDIT. where the period specifies the last used line number. This saves typing in the line number.

THE L COMMAND

The L command is used to see the line being edited. Type L and BASIC will print out line 100, print 100 on the next line, and stop. Thus anytime you type L, BASIC will display the rest of the line and start over again. Any changes you made to the line before you typed L are retained. This also permits you to see the result of any changes you made to the line while retaining the line in the EDIT mode.

THE I COMMAND

The I command is used to insert material within an already typed line. The I stands for insert and adds any characters you enter after the I to the line starting at the cursor position. To get out of the I mode, use the ESCAPE key or CR (carriage return or ENTER key). The ESCAPE key will get you out of the insert mode, but you will retain your position in the line being edited. If you use CR you will leave the insert mode and the remainder of the line will be displayed. To get the line back for further editing, use the EDIT. command.

THE SPACE KEY

Here is one more thing before we give some examples. After you type EDIT 100 (or whatever line number), for every space you type, a successive character from line 100 will be displayed. This way you can type spaces until you reach the point where you wish to edit. Thus, if in the line

10 PRINT "THIS IS END"

you wish to add THE between IS and END, type EDIT 10, then type spaces until you get to the S in IS. Now type I to put BASIC into the insert mode. Type a space, then THE, then a CR. This will result in

10 PRINT "THIS IS THE END"

You can also prefix the space with an integer value, and EDIT will move you that number of characters.

THE Q COMMAND

If you make a mistake and wish to abort the edit, type Q for quit. Typing Q will get you out of the edit mode. BASIC will retain the old unedited line, or at least the version of the line before you last typed EDIT.

Note: while you can use delete or rubout characters while in the edit mode, control-C will not work.

THE X COMMAND

The X command is used for another type of insert operation. This permits you to add characters to the end of the line. To use it, get the line with the EDIT command, then enter X. The entire line will be displayed and you will automatically be placed in the insert (I) mode. Now enter the material you wished to add to the end of the line; type a CR to exit.

THE H COMMAND

The H command is used for another type of insert operation where you wish to replace the last part of a line. To use this, type spaces (or use the S command described later) until you reach the point in the line where you wish to begin the new material. Typing H will delete the part of the line following the cursor and place you in the insert (I) mode. Now type in your new material and type CR to exit.

THE D COMMAND

The D command is used for deleting characters. Use the space bar (or S command) to reach the point where you wish to make the deletion. Then type D to delete the character. If you wish to delete three characters, use 3D, the deleted characters will be placed within backslashes to show they were deleted.

THE S COMMAND

The S command mentioned earlier, is used to quickly reach a point in a line. It is faster than using the space bar. To use it, type S followed by the character you wish to reach. The computer will display the line up to but not including the first occurrence of the character following the S. If the character also appears before the desired position, type a digit in front of the S to determine which occurrence of the letter you are interested in. The search begins at the second character after the cursor position when you enter the S. Here's an example.

```
10 PRINT "AND SO WE EDIT"
EDIT 10
10 2SD (CR)
10 PRINT "AND SO WE E
```

Now you can select the I, H, or D command to select the edit function you wish. You can also combine edit commands, for example,

```
10 PRINT "AND SO WE DIT"
EDIT 10
10 2SDIE (CR)
```

This will result in adding the letter E before the DIT and finishing the line display.

THE K COMMAND

The K command is something like the S command, but it deletes all the characters passed over. These characters are displayed between backslashes to indicate that they have been deleted.

To use the K command, type K followed by the character you wish to delete to. All characters from the cursor position to the character following the K will be deleted.

THE C COMMAND

The C command is used to change characters in the line being edited. To use it, use the space bar or S to get to the character before the character you wish to change, then type C, followed by the new character. The old character will be replaced by the one following the C. To change several characters, type the number of characters you wish to change directly in front of the C, and enter the new characters.

When in the edit mode the command characters, including any digits and characters you add to them, are not echoed to the terminal. That is, when you type, for example, CY, the C does not appear on the terminal, but the new character, the Y, does. Also, if you enter 2SE, the 2SE will not be displayed, but the portion of the line being edited up to the second appearance of an E will be displayed.

EXITING AN EDITED LINE:
THE E AND A COMMANDS

Earlier we mentioned that a CR will display the remainder of the line you are editing and return you to the BASIC command mode. There are several other ways to exit a line being edited.

The E command means the same as the CR, except that the remainder of the line is not displayed. The material still exists in the edited line, it is just not displayed.

The Q command permits you to exit an edited line and disregards all the edits you may have made since the last time you used EDIT. It is usually used if you change your mind about editing that line, or have really botched up the line.

The L command causes the remainder of the line to be displayed, retains any edits made, and prints the line number again so you can continue editing the line.

The A command, like Q, deletes the edits made but prints the line number so you can edit the line again.

If you are running a program and get a SYNTAX ERROR, BASIC automatically goes into the edit mode and prints the line number of the line containing the error. To see the line and then edit it, type L. Editing a line while the program is running causes all variable values to be lost. If you wish to examine any of these values before you edit, type Q after BASIC goes into the edit mode after a SYNTAX ERROR. Then all the variables will be retained.

USING CONTROL-A

If you are entering a line in the normal command mode and wish to edit the line before you reach the CR at the end of the line, enter control-A. This will restart the line in the edit mode. In this case a ! will be displayed on the next line instead of the line number, permitting you to edit the line number, too, if you wish.

SOME EXAMPLES

Here are a few examples of the use of the edit commands.

```
10 FOR X = 1 TO Y : A(X) = 0 : GOTO 170
```

Let's say you want to change this by adding STEP .1, changing the line number after the GOTO to 1700, and changing A(X) = 0 to A(X) = 1.

Type <u>EDIT 10</u>
10
Now type <u>S:</u>
10 FOR X = 1 TO Y
Now type <u>ISTEP .1</u> (ESCAPE)
10 FOR X = 1 TO Y STEP .1
Now type <u>S0</u>
10 FOR X = 1 TO Y STEP .1 : A(X) =
Type <u>C1</u>
10 FOR X = 1 TO Y STEP .1 : A(X) = 1
Type <u>X</u>
10 FOR X = 1 TO Y STEP .1 : A(X) = 1 : GOTO 170
You are now in the I mode, so type 0 (followed by a CR).
10 FOR X = 1 TO Y STEP .1 : A(X) = 1 : GOTO 1700
And there it is!

Here's another.

100 A = 0 : IF X = Y AND Z = 4 THEN 240 ELSE 260

Let's say you wish to delete the A = 0, the AND Z = 4, and the ELSE 260.

Type <u>KI</u>
\A = 0 : \
Type <u>SA</u>
\A = 0 : \IF X = Y
Type <u>8D</u>
\A = 0 : \IF X = Y\ AND Z = 4\
Type <u>2SE</u>
\A = 0 : \IF X = Y\ AND Z = 4\ THEN 240
Type H (CR) and you are finished.

If you have EXTENDED BASIC, try editing a few lines to get the feel of it. Especially use the S command, as it saves typing a lot of spaces. If you miscount the number of repetitions of the desired letter and go past your destination, just type L and try again. You can use the delete, rubout, or whatever to back up to your edit point if you only overshoot it by a few characters.

When there are more characters than you can count at a glance to delete, make an estimate you think is a little smaller than the actual count and use D. Now you should have few enough characters remaining to be deleted to count easily.

Note that ESCAPE means the key marked ESCAPE on your keyboard. This key might be labeled ALTMODE on some keyboards.

If you enter an invalid command character, BASIC will let you know with a bell or a beep. This will have no effect on the edited line.

Chapter Seven

Arrays and Files

ARRAYS

A very convenient way to handle groups of related data in a program is to use an array. An array is a list or matrix containing related data. For example, a list of names and quantities used in an inventory list could be logically organized as an array. The array would look something like this:

```
A(1) 35
A(2) 42
A(3) 21
```

Imagine that A(1) refers to Corn Flakes and 35 to the number of boxes of Corn Flakes in inventory; A(2) to Rice Puffs with 42 boxes in inventory; and A(3) to Tootie Fruities with 21 boxes in storage. There are many more examples.

One-dimensional arrays

An array must be dimensioned before it can be used. This is accomplished using the DIM (8K) statement. The syntax is DIM X(Y) where X is the array name and Y is the number of elements in the array. DIM A(10) can mean a maximum of 10 or 11 numeric items associated with array A. (The maximum depends on whether OPTION BASE 1 is used; this is discussed in a moment.) Note that A(X) and A are two different variables and can be used in the same program. For example:

```
10 A = 10 : DIM A(20)
20 A(A) = 17
```

Though legal, I'd try to avoid this as it can be rather confusing. At any rate, A = 10 and A(A) (or A(10)) = 17. The element designator (10 in this case) is called the *subscript*. The subscript specifies the exact element of the array being referenced.

Before we go any further, we should mention a feature called OPTION BASE (8K). This permits the first subscript in an array to be either 0 or 1. Note that this sets the minimum subscript value to 0 or 1 for ALL the arrays, not just one or a selected few. If you prefer to work with arays that start with a subscript of 1 rather than 0, then use

```
OPTION BASE 1
```

The default is 0. You should declare the OPTION BASE before you DIM the arrays. In the rest of the book we will assume that we have not used OPTION BASE, and all arrays therefore begin with a zero element. OPTION BASE 1 is the reason we said earlier that DIM A(10) could have a maximum of 10 or 11 elements. DIM A(10) will have 10 elements with OPTION BASE 1; the subscripts will be (1) to (10). Without OPTION BASE 1, DIM A(10) will have 11 elements, with subscripts from (0) to (10).

If an array is not explicitly dimensioned but is referenced in the program, the maximum value of the subscript(s) (number of elements) is set to 10. This means you can use A(X) for 11 variables, A(0) through A(10), in the following program

```
10 X = 5 : A(X) = 100
```

since A was not DIMed. If we had a line 20

```
20 Y = 12 : A(Y) = 200
```

we would get a SUBSCRIPT OUT OF RANGE error, since by not explicitly DIMing A, we set the maximum subscript value to 10 (by default); the Y (12) in line 20 refers to an element out of this range. If line 20 was

```
20 DIM A(12) : Y = 12 : A(Y) = 200
```

we would still be in trouble. The DIM A(12) would get us a DOUBLE DIMENSION error since line 10 DIMed (by default) the A array to 10.

DIMing by default is legal in BASIC, but it is better to explicitly set the array values with DIM statements. This saves confusion when trying to decipher the program at a later date; it also can save memory. For example, if you do not DIM an array and you use a maximum subscript of 5, you are wasting the memory dedicated to elements 6 through 10. They are available whether you use them or not. If you previously DIMed the array to 5, then that memory would not be wasted. If the array was double precision you would be wasting 40 bytes of memory by not DIMing the array. This is not much, but it all adds up!

Once an array is DIMed, its size is fixed for the entire program — unless you use ERASE (EXTENDED). ERASE A will erase array A just as if you had not previously used it in the program. To reuse it just DIM it again or use it with the maximum subscript of 10 default.

```
ERASE A, B, C
```

will ERASE arrays A, B, and C. Note that this is the only way you can reDIM an array in a program, and in 8K there is no way to reDIM an array. If you try to reDIM without using ERASE you will get a DOUBLE DIMENSION error. This also means that if you have a program with a DIM statement in it, and the program restarts itself (perhaps a game is repeated), you must be careful not to go through the lines containing the DIM statement(s) again or you'll get the error. You can't even reDIM an array to its previous size.

The DIM statement automatically sets all the array elements to 0, or " " (null) if a string array. Also, if you wish to DIM more than one array at the same time you can include them in a single DIM statement separated by commas. For example,

```
10 DIM A(12),B(25),C # (100),D%(5)
```

or whatever. It is best to define all the arrays at once early in the program so that if the program branches back to the beginning, you can easily arrange to skip that line and avoid the DOUBLE DIMENSION error.

Arrays of More than One Dimension

An array set to A(20) is called a one-dimensional array. You can set up as many dimensions as will fit on a line, but you will probably run out of memory before you get very far. Thus, DIM B(2,2,2,2) is a four-dimensional array. Normally two dimensions, occasionally three, are as high as you will go. An example of a two-dimensional array is

```
10 DIM A(4,3)
20 FOR X = 1 TO 4
30 FOR Y = 1 TO 3
40 A(X,Y) = Y
50 NEXT Y,X
```

This will result in

A(0,0)	A(0,1)	A(0,2)	A(0,3)
0	0	0	0
A(1,0)	A(1,1)	A(1,2)	A(1,3)
0	1	2	3
A(2,0)	A(2,1)	A(2,2)	A(2,3)
0	1	2	3
A(3,0)	A(3,1)	A(3,2)	A(3,3)
0	1	2	3
A(4,0)	A(4,1)	A(4,2)	A(4,3)
0	1	2	3

Another possibility is

```
10 Z = 0 : DIM A(4,3)
20 FOR X = 1 TO 4
30 FOR Y = 1 TO 3
40 Z = Z + 1
50 A(X,Y) = Z
60 NEXT Y,X
```

resulting in

```
0    0    0    0
0    1    2    3
0    4    5    6
0    7    8    9
0   10   11   12
```

Note the eight wasted elements in each array (the ones set to 0). Remember, the 0 subscript (unless you use OPTION BASE 1) specifies a valid element in the array in every dimension.

More About Arrays

Arrays can take up lots of memory. The statement

```
DIM (100,100)
```

will use 40,804 bytes (4 bytes per element, 100*101 elements, with 804 bytes used for the 0 subscripts!). Be careful not to reserve more space than you need (remember, once you DIM an array the space is reserved whether you use it or not).

You can also use integer or double precision arrays. DIM A%(10) (EXTENDED) defines an integer array or DIM A#(20) defines a double precision array. Obviously, you can only store integers in an integer array.

As you have noticed in the examples, you can use variables to define an array's size.

```
10 A = 10 : B = 20 : DIM C(A,B)
```

Also, the variable need not be an integer, but will automatically be truncated to one. Thus if

```
10 A = 10.5 : B = 20.9 : DIM C(A,B)
```

then array C will be DIMed to C(10,20).

It goes without saying that you can't use negative numbers to set the array size: DIM A(-10) will not work.

As you might have guessed, strings can also be put in arrays.

Thus DIM A$(12) defines a thirteen element string array (remember the 0 element). As with numeric storage, you can use multiple dimensions. String elements in an array can be up to 255 characters long. The strings themselves are stored in string space, so the CLEAR statement must provide room for the anticipated strings.

Arrays have many uses, especially where the data is related. Here's an example of one such use of an array. We want to put a deck of 52 cards in an array, shuffle them, and deal two 10-card hands.

```
10 DIM CD(52,2),CH(20,1),PH(10,1)
20 CT = 1 : A = 1
30 FOR X = 1 TO 52
40 CT = CT + 1
50 CD(X,0) = CT : CD(X,1) = A
60 IF CT/14 = INT(CT/14) THEN CT = 1 : A = A + 1
70 NEXT
80 FOR X = 1 TO 20
90 R = INT (52*RND(1) + 1)
100 IF CD(R,2) = 1 THEN 90
110 CH(X,0) = CD(R,0) : CH(X,1) = CD(R,1) : CD(R,2) = 1
120 NEXT
130 FOR X = 1 TO 52
140 CD(X,2) = 0
150 NEXT
160 FOR X = 1 TO 10
170 PH(X,0) = CH(X + 10,0) : PH(X,1) = CH(X + 10,1)
180 NEXT
```

The description of the program's operation follows.

10) We dimension the three arrays we are using.
20) We initialize the counters. CT is the card number and A is the suit number.
30) Set up a 52 card FOR loop.
40) Set CT to 2 (we are using 14 for the ace).
50) Put CT and A in the CD array.
60) Test for the end of each group of 14 cards. If we are at the end of a group then we have completed a suit. We then increment A to the next suit and set CT to 1 again.
70) Go to next count in the FOR loop.

We now have the following array set up.

CD(1,0)	CD(1,1)	CD(1,2)
2	1	0
CD(2,0)	CD(2,1)	CD(2,2)
3	1	0
CD(3,0)	CD(3,1)	CD(3,2)
4	1	0

CD(12,0)	CD(12,1)	CD(12,2)
13	1	0
CD(13,0)	CD(13,1)	CD(13,2)
14	1	0
CD(14,0)	CD(14,1)	CD(14,2)
2	2	0
CD(15,0)	CD(15,1)	CD(15,2)
3	2	0

CD(25,0)	CD(25,1)	CD(25,2)
13	2	0
CD(26,0)	CD(26,1)	CD(26,2)
14	2	0
CD(27,0)	CD(27,1)	CD(27,2)
1	3	0

Until we get to

CD(51,0)	CD(51,1)	CD(51,2)
13	4	0
CD(52,0)	CD(52,1)	CD(52,2)
14	4	0

We now have the deck in the CD array. The next step is to deal the two hands. To make it easier, we'll deal one hand of 20 cards, then split it in two.

80) We set up a 20 count FOR loop.
90) We get a random integer between 1 and 52.
100) We check to see if we used that card (see line 110).
110) We put the card chosen by the random number R into the next CH(X,0) array element. We put the suit in CH(X,1) and set CD(R,2) to 1 to show that card is used.
120) Next X.

We now have 20 random cards with their suit in array CH. The next step is to go through array CD and put a 0 in all the third elements so next time we deal the card will be available again.

130) Set up a 52 card FOR loop.
140) Set the third dimensional element in CD to 0.
150) Next X.

Next we split the 20-card hand in CH into two 10-card hands.

160) A 10 count FOR loop.
170) Move cards from CH array to PH array, starting at card 11 in the CH array.
180) Next X.

We now have two random hands of 10 cards in arrays CH and PH with no duplicate cards. (Actually we have 20 cards in the CH array but in the game we won't use the last 10 we moved to the PH array.)

As the game progresses and we need to print out card names and suits we could use an ON...GOSUB or an ON...GOTO statement to get the card name and suit name.

If you have EXTENDED BASIC, change X to X%, and the program will speed up substantially. If you add a % to all the variables, things will go even faster, and the array CD%( ) will only take up half the space.

So there's one use for arrays. Note how we kept the card value, suit, and used flag together by using a three element per card array.

We could have put the card names and suit names directly into the deck or hand arrays by using string arrays but that approach would have several disadvantages. It would use much more memory and in the course of the game it would make comparing card values and suits much more difficult.

You might also note we did some calculating with the array subscripts in line 70 (CH(X + 10,0)). This is perfectly legal and can be very useful. The array element subscripts can be any positive number (up to 65535, not necessarily an integer), a variable name, or a formula.

To calculate memory overhead for the arrays in your programs use

```
INTEGER           2*E + 2*D + 6
SINGLE PRECISION  4*E + 2*D + 6
DOUBLE PRECISION  8*E + 2*D + 6
STRING            3*E + 2*D + 6
```

If a string, add the string space required by the string. The array only points to the location of the strings; it does not contain them. Numeric variables, however, are contained in the arrays; no added space is required. In the above table, E stands for the number of elements in the array, D stands for the number of dimensions. Thus B(50,3) would require 826 bytes of memory (4*(51*4) + 2*2 + 6), B%(20,5,3) would require 1020 bytes (2*(21*6*4) + 2*3 + 6), and B#(80) would need 656 bytes (8*81 + 2*1 + 6).

FILES

There are several types of files in BASIC. The primary type is called the *program file* and contains the programming lines and line numbers we have been discussing so far in this book. The other type of file is called a *data file* and comes in two types, *sequential* and *random access*. The two types of files are described in detail in the next chapter.

What we are interested in here are program files and cassette machines. In some versions of Microsoft BASIC, depending on the computer system, you have the option of storing your programs on cassette tape.

To store the BASIC program on tape, type in CSAVE "PROG1" where PROG1 is the name you chose for your program. In this case BASIC only uses the first letter, or the P, as the program name. Be sure your cassette recorder is in the record mode and is recording before you press the CR key. Make sure you are past the plastic tape leader if you are at the beginning of a cassette. Some computers will start the cassette machine for you. BASIC will give you an OK when the recording is complete. It is usually a good idea to save the program several times in case one save is defective.

To check the recording, return the tape to the same spot where the recording began. Now type in CLOAD? "P". Roll the tape in play mode. If you get an OK from BASIC after the program has been read, it is good. If BASIC displays NO GOOD, then it is just that. Try a different playback volume setting and try again. Be aware, tape is slow and the playback volume setting is critical.

To get back the program use CLOAD "P". You will find out if the retrieve was successful when you try to LIST or RUN the program. In some computers you are told if the CLOAD was unsuccessful. The CLOAD does a NEW when it loads the program so any previous program in memory is wiped out.

CSAVE, CLOAD, and CLOAD? are only usable as direct commands. You can't use them in a program line. The following tape command can be used in a program.

To save a numerical array on tape use CSAVE* A, where the array name is A. To get the array back use CLOAD* A. Here's an example to help make this clear.

```
 90........
100 INPUT "START RECORDER IN RECORD MODE, THEN PRESS
    THE CR KEY";A$
110 FOR X = 1 TO 1000 : NEXT
120 REM TIME TO LET THE RECORDER COME UP TO SPEED
130 CSAVE* A
140 INPUT "STOP RECORDER AND REWIND TO USE ARRAY,
    THEN PRESS THE CR KEY";A$
150........
```

To CLOAD A use

```
200........
210 INPUT "START RECORDER IN PLAY, THEN PRESS CR KEY";
    A$
220 CLOAD* A
230 INPUT "STOP RECORDER, THEN PRESS CR KEY";A$
240........
```

In the above program it is assumed that the array A is loaded with the data before line 100, and the routine beginning with line 200 assumes that the array A had been DIMed sometime before line 210. You must use the same array variable when CLOAD* is used as was used with CSAVE*.

When BASIC CSAVE*s an array, it saves the first dimension first, then the next element in the second dimension, etc. For example, in an array set to DIM A(3,3) it saves in this order:

A(0,0), A(1,0), A(2,0), A(3,0), A(0,1), A(1,1), A(2,1), A(3,1),
A(0,2), A(1,2), A(2,2), A(3,2), A(0,3), A(1,3), A(2,3), A(3,3)

If you wished, you could change the array before you CLOAD*ed it by

```
10 DIM A(3,3)
. . . . . . . . .
50 CSAVE* A
60 ERASE A
70 DIM A(15)
80 CLOAD* A
. . . . . . . . .
```

thereby saving a two dimensional array and retrieving it as a single dimension array. Remember, BASIC just stores 16 numbers on tape with the file name A; it doesn't care how you store them when you read them back, just so long as there is room enough to store all the numbers saved on tape and an array with the proper name is DIMed.

Note: I left out the operator instructions to make the program easier to understand. In a real program, unless the computer controlled the tape recorder, they would be necessary.

Chapter Eight

The Disk

A floppy disk drive is a most useful peripheral for a microcomputer system. The floppy disk can be used as a huge memory, allows program files to be saved and loaded quickly and easily, stores data files whose contents change from one run of the program to the next, permits very fast access for recording and retrieving file data, allows loading and running programs in segments when the complete program is too large to load into memory at one time, permits saving and using very large arrays without using main memory, and many other possibilities you will invent as you use the disk. We will discuss some of these uses in this chapter.

Before we go any further, note that all commands in this chapter are found only in DISK BASIC.

At this point it might be well to mention that floppy diskettes are, in some ways, rather fragile. To help preserve their health, here's a list of don'ts:

1) Don't touch the surface of the diskette. Always handle the envelope instead.
2) Don't let the diskette get near any magnetic source. Examples: magnetized paper clips, motors (vacuum cleaner, electric pencil sharpener, etc.), telephone, power supplies, transformers, fans, CRT terminals, line printers, etc.
3) Don't bend, fold, staple, or mutilate the diskette. When mailing a diskette be very careful to protect it.
4) Don't write directly on the diskette envelope. If you must write on an attached label, use a felt tip pen and a very light touch.

5) Don't let the diskette collect any dust in storage; keep it well covered.
6) Don't turn your system on or off with diskettes in the drives. Don't store diskettes in the drives.
7) Don't smoke around open diskettes or the disk drives.

If you get a DISK I/O error, it could be a speck of dust on the diskette or a damaged diskette. Usually there is no recovery of that file. Sometimes the diskette (but not its data) can be recovered by formatting it again. Frequently make backup copies of your valued diskettes or files in case something happens to the original. Special programs are available to attempt saving a defective file.

Programs and data are stored on diskettes as files. The exact manner in which data is stored sometimes differs from one computer to another, so diskettes are frequently not interchangeable between different computer brands and different disk operating systems.

SAVING AND LOADING BASIC PROGRAMS

BASIC programs are stored as files. Assuming you have a BASIC program in your computer, you must first select a name for the program. The name must be different from any other file name on that diskette. The rules for forming names vary from DOS (disk operating system) to DOS. We will assume it can be a word up to eight characters long. Let's name the program PROG1. To save it on diskette use

```
SAVE "PROG1"
```

If you have more than one disk drive, you might need to add a number after the program name to direct it to a specific drive. Check your DOS documentation. In our examples we will assume you only have one drive.

Normally, a BASIC program is stored as a *binary file*, using abbreviations for BASIC words, groups of spaces, etc. If you wish to SAVE the program on the diskette exactly as written, for example when the program is to be used as data by another progam, perhaps the Microsoft BASIC compiler, use

```
SAVE "PROG1",A
```

This means that the program is being saved as an *ASCII file*, rather than as a binary file. Note that this will take up more room on the diskette and takes much longer to SAVE and LOAD. Normally you wouldn't use this option. If you wish to *protect* a program from being listed or edited, SAVE it with

```
SAVE "PROG1",P
```

Note that this protects the program against you too, so be sure to save another copy of the program on another diskette, or under a different name, without the P suffix. That way you can list and edit it if need be.

To get the program back off the diskette use

```
LOAD "PROG1"
```

PROG1 will now replace any BASIC program that was in the computer. To add PROG1 to a BASIC program already in memory use

```
MERGE "PROG1"
```

Note that the two BASIC programs must have different line numbers. If the original program has the same line number as one in the MERGEd program, the original line will be lost, replaced by the new line.

Once a program is LOADed you must type RUN to start it. To eliminate this hardship you can use

```
RUN "PROG1"
```

This will LOAD and RUN PROG1.

Here's one last option. If you want to have one program LOAD another program and RUN it, you can either use the previous RUN "PROG1" as a statement in the program, or use

```
RUN "PROG1",R
```

in a program line. If any data files were OPEN in the calling program, they will remain OPEN when the new program RUNs. Normally all data files are CLOSEd when a new program is LOADed.

ERASING FILES

To erase a program or data file, PROG1 for example, use

```
KILL "PROG1"
```

Be careful! Once you KILL a file you can't get it back under most DOS's! Also, don't KILL an OPEN data file.

RENAMING FILES

If you wish to change the name of a program or data file already on a diskette use

```
NAME "OLDFILE" AS "NEWFILE"
```

where OLDFILE is the old file name and NEWFILE the new one.

DATA FILES

Here is where a disk drive can really be useful. Data files come in two flavors, as mentioned in the previous chapter. There are sequential access files and random access files. Some data lends itself to sequential files, and other data to random files. Each has its use.

SEQUENTIAL FILES

Sequential files are easier to create, if you are careful how you store the data, but they must always be read by starting at the beginning of the file and reading sequentially to the data you want or until the end of the file is reached. If you always wish to read all the data (storing arrays for example), this is the way to go. If you are not sure how many items are going to be in a file, are not sure in what order the data will be stored, are not sure of the exact lengths of each item of data, and if you will not wish to change, add, or delete any of the data on the diskette, then sequential files will probably be your best bet.

We'll write a little program to illustrate, then explain it. Be sure to follow through this example, and the two following, as many of the command descriptions are imbedded in the explanations.

```
10 CLEAR 500
20 PRINT "THIS PROGRAM IS USED TO STORE NAMES AND"
30 PRINT "TELEPHONE NUMBERS."
40 PRINT: PRINT "MENU"
50 PRINT "1: CREATE A LIST"
60 PRINT "2: RETRIEVE A NAME"
70 PRINT "3: FINISH THE PROGRAM"
80 INPUT "YOUR CHOICE";A : IF A<1 OR A>3 THEN PRINT
   "BAD CHOICE" : GOTO 80
90 ON A GOTO 110,180,100
100 END
110 OPEN "O",1,"TELEFONE"
120 LINE INPUT "NAME (USE 'DONE' TO FINISH)? ";A$
130 IF A$ = "DONE" THEN 170
140 LINE INPUT "NUMBER? ";B$
150 PRINT #1,CHR$(34);A$;CHR$(34);",";CHR$(34);
    B$;CHR$(34)
160 GOTO 120
170 CLOSE : GOTO 40
180 OPEN "I",1,"TELEFONE"
190 LINE INPUT "NAME (USE 'DONE' TO FINISH)? ";A$
200 IF EOF(1) THEN 260
210 LINE INPUT #1,A$,B$
220 IF A$<>C$ THEN 200
230 PRINT "NAME ";A$
240 PRINT "PHONE NUMBER ";B$
250 GOTO 270
260 PRINT "NAME ";C$;" NOT FOUND"
270 CLOSE: GOTO 40
```

Line 10 CLEARs string space for the names and phone numbers. Line 80 gets the menu choice, repeating the request if the response is invalid. Line 90 selects the proper part of the program to perform the menu choice. Line 100 is for menu selection 3 and ENDs the program.

Lines 110 to 170 store the names and phone numbers in the sequential file "TELEFONE". Line 110 OPENs the file "TELEFONE" for writing. If this file already existed on the diskette, its contents are now gone forever. This is important! Opening a sequential file with "O" wipes out everything already there and begins anew. (We'll tell you how to get around this at the end of the section on sequential files.) The "O" selects writing for the that file ("O" stands for output from the computer to the disk). The 1 is the file number. The total number of files you can have OPEN at one time is determined by how you start BASIC from the disk. See your operating system and BASIC documentation.

Line 120 gets the name to be associated with the phone number. LINE INPUT to the variable A$ is used in case the name contains a comma. Note that we added the question mark and the space following it to the prompt. In line 130 we check to see if the entries are completed. If not, we go on to line 140 and get the phone number.

In line 150 we write the name and phone number into file #1. Note the "," and CHR$(34)'s between the variables. This is necessary to separate them in the file because the strings may contain commas. More about this later. Then, in line 160, we got back to line 120 to get another name and number or finish the input.

If we found the word DONE in A$ in line 130 we jump to line 170, CLOSE the file, and return to the menu. Using CLOSE by itself CLOSEs all OPEN files. If we wanted to CLOSE specific files, we would use their file number(s) after the command: CLOSE 1 CLOSEs only file #1; CLOSE 1, 2, 4 CLOSEs files 1, 2, and 4; and so on. We could have used CLOSE 1 in line 170. Always CLOSE a file after you finish with it. It must be CLOSEd to switch between reading and writing.

Lines 180 through 270 are used to read the file. In line 180 we OPEN the file "TELEFONE" to read it. The "I" stands for input to the computer from the disk. The 1 is the line number.

Line 190 gets the name for which we want the phone number.

Line 200 is important. It checks to see if there is any more data in the file. EOF stands for end of file and the number in parentheses is the file number. If we have read to the end of the file, we must not have found a matching name. If this is

the case we go to line 260 to advise the user of that fact, then
to line 270 to CLOSE the file, then back to the menu. We must
CLOSE the file after reading from it so we will start at the
beginning of the file next time we read it with another OPEN
"I". If we try to OPEN it again without first CLOSEing it, we'll
get an error.

In line 210 we get back a name and phone number. Note
that we use LINE INPUT #1 to read the file because we stored
data we got with a LINE INPUT in lines 120 and 140. If we
had used INPUT in lines 120 and 140 we'd use INPUT #1 in
line 210.

In line 220 we check the name we got from the file, in A$,
against the name we are searching the file for, in C$. If there
is no match we got back to line 200 to get another name and
number, or CLOSE the file.

We "fall through" to line 230 if A$ = C$ in line 220. We then
display the name with line 230 and the phone number with
line 240. Then in line 250 we jump to line 270 (to skip line 260
which is not valid now), CLOSE the file, and return to the
menu.

We put numbers in a sequential file in almost the same way,
using numeric variables. When storing numeric variables you
don't need to use the "," between the variables. Thus:

```
PRINT #1,A#;B!;C%;D
```

We retrieve them with

```
INPUT #1,E#,F!,G%,H
```

Note that we do not need to use the same variable names to
store and retrieve. It is, however, a good idea to use the same
variable type.

We can mix strings and numbers.

```
PRINT #1,A;B;C$
```

If we get our string data with INPUT instead of LINE IN-
PUT, then we need not use the CHR$(34)'s. Thus:

```
PRINT #1,A$;",";B$;",";C$
```

Don't forget the EOF (file number). If it is not used there is always the chance of trying to read past the end of the file and crashing the program.

We can use PRINT USING to store a formatted string and/or number in a file.

```
PRINT # 1, USING "###.##,";A,B,C
```

Note the comma after the number signs (#). This separates the formatted numbers in the file.

Strings are written to a sequential file as they would be printed. So

```
A$ = "NAME"
B$ = "NUMBER"
PRINT #1,A$;B$
```

would put the information on the disk as it would be printed. So:

```
NAMENUMBER
```

I suspect this is not what you had in mind, because now we have no way of separating the two words when we retrieve them. The statement

```
PRINT #1,A$;",";B$
```

puts them on the disk as

```
NAME,NUMBER
```

and, since the comma is a string delimiter (separator), they can now be retrieved as two strings. However, if the string contains a comma or other string delimiter, we must use quotation marks to separate the strings. CHR$(34) is used to produce the quote marks.

```
A$ = "JOHN PAUL, JR "
B$ = "782-5678, EXT. 128"
PRINT #1,CHR$(34);A$;CHR$(34);",";CHR$(34);B$;CHR$(34)
```

would store them on the disk as

"JOHN PAUL, JR", "782-5678, EXT. 128"

which will keep the JOHN PAUL and the JR together in a single variable when we retrieve it. If we didn't separate them using CHR$(34), they'd be on disk as

JOHN PAUL, JR,782-5678, EXT. 128

and it would require four variables to retrieve them. To avoid problems you should be careful when using PRINT # to write your strings to the disk.

We have not yet mentioned the file command LOC(X). It is used with sequential files to find out how many 128 byte disk sectors have been allocated to file number X since it was OPENed. (With random access files it returns the number of records, rather than sectors.)

```
200 IF LOC(3)>50 THEN 500
```

Last, but not least, be aware than you can't add data to a sequential file once it has been CLOSEd. When you use OPEN "O" to write to the file, any data that was in it is now gone. You must copy the data to another file, then add to it.

```
10 CLEAR 500 : OPEN "I",1,"ORIGINAL" : OPEN "O",2,"COPY"
20 IF EOF(1) THEN 60
30 INPUT #1,A$
40 PRINT #2,A$
50 GOTO 20
60 INPUT "ADDED DATA";A$
70 PRINT #2,A$
80 CLOSE
90 KILL "ORIGINAL"
100 NAME "COPY" AS "ORIGINAL"
```

We are assuming all the data in the file is stored as strings in this example. We also assume you only intend to add one data string to the end of the file. Note that we had to KILL "ORIGINAL" before we could reuse the file name in line 100.

RANDOM FILES

Random access files are a little more difficult to handle than sequential files. However, if you wish to go directly to any specific data item, you can do so. You can also change data in a file, delete data, or add more data to the end of a random file.

You can only store strings in a random file; no numbers are allowed. However, you can store numbers by first converting them to strings. There are two ways to do this. Use X$ = STR$(X) to change X to a string before you store it, and X = VAL(X$) to change the string back to a number after you retrieve it from the file. This will work, but is not recommended. Why not?

1) It is slow.
2) The resulting string is liable to be any length, depending on the number of digits in the number, presence of a decimal point, etc.

Here's a much better way. For integers use X$ = MKI$(X%). To convert back to the number use X% = CVI(X$). This string is always two bytes long, no matter how many digits there are in the number.

For single precision numbers use X$ = MKS$(X). To convert back to the number use X = CVS(X$). This string is always four bytes long.

For double precision numbers use X$ = MKD$(X#). To convert back to the number use X# = CVD(X$). This string is always eight bytes long.

When using this method the number must be a pure number, not formatted with PRINT USING or containing dashes, commas, dollar signs, etc. Of course it can contain a decimal point (unless an integer), and can be in E or D format (1.23E + 14). If an integer it must be within the allowable integer size range of − 32768 to 32767.

Random files are organized as *records*. Usually each record is 128 bytes long (see your documentation for possible exceptions). Each record is identified with a number, from 1 to the allowable maximum number of records there is room for on the diskette. To save and retrieve a record, the record number must be used.

Records can be divided into *subrecords*. You determine the
size of the subrecords and how many there are with the
FIELD statement.
The word GET is used to retrieve a record; the word PUT is
used to store a record. Before you PUT a record you must use
LSET or RSET to assign the data to the record.
To OPEN a random access file use OPEN "R"; to CLOSE it
use the usual CLOSE.
Now that you know all about random records, let's create
a simple random version of the previous telephone number
program.

```
10 CLEAR 500 : OPEN "R",1,"TELEFONE"
20 FIELD 1,25 AS A$,25 AS B$
30 PRINT "THIS PROGRAM IS USED TO STORE NAMES AND"
40 PRINT "PHONE NUMBERS." : PRINT
50 PRINT "MENU"
60 PRINT "1: ADD A NAME"
70 PRINT "2: RETRIEVE A NAME"
80 PRINT "3: CHANGE A NAME OR NUMBER"
90 PRINT "4: DELETE A NAME"
100 PRINT "5: FINISH"
110 INPUT "YOUR CHOICE";A : IF A<1 OR A>5 THEN PRINT
    "BAD CHOICE" : GOTO 110
120 ON A GOTO 140,190,220,280,130
130 CLOSE : END
140 C = LOF(1) + 1
150 GOSUB 400 : GOSUB 500
160 LSET A$ = N$ : LSET B$ = P$
170 PUT 1,C
180 GOTO 50
190 GOSUB 400
200 GOSUB 1000
210 GOTO 50
220 PRINT "ENTER NAME TO CHANGE"
230 GOSUB 400
240 GOSUB 1000
250 IF FL = 1 THEN 50
260 PRINT "ENTER NEW INFORMATION"
270 GOTO 150
280 PRINT "ENTER NAME TO DELETE"
290 GOSUB 400
```

```
300 GOSUB 1000
310 IF FL=1 THEN 50
320 N$=" "
330 GOTO 160

400 LINE INPUT "NAME? ";N$
410 IF LEN(N$)>25 THEN PRINT "TOO LONG" : GOTO 400
420 RETURN

500 LINE INPUT "PHONE NUMBER? ";P$
510 IF LEN(P$)>25 THEN PRINT "TOO LONG" : GOTO 500
520 RETURN

1000 C=0 : FL=0
1010 C=C+1
1020 IF C>LOF(1) THEN 1060
1030 GET 1,C
1040 IF A$=LEFT$ (N$ SPACE$(24),25) THEN 1070
1050 GOTO 1010
1060 PRINT N$;" NOT FOUND" : FL=1 : GOTO 1090
1070 PRINT "NAME ";A$
1080 PRINT "PHONE ";B$
1090 RETURN
```

Line 10 CLEARs a string area for the string data and OPENs the file. Note that we use "R" for a random file.

Line 20 is the FIELD statement. The data that is to be stored in a record is organized in a buffer with this statement. The FIELD statement sets the amount of space reserved for each string variable in the record. In this case a 1 followed FIELD, meaning that this FIELD statement is to be associated with file #1 (OPENed in line 10). The 25 AS A$ reserved 25 bytes for the data to be associated with the string variable A$, and 25 AS B$ did the same for B$. Do not use the variables declared in a FIELD statement elsewhere in a program (except for LSET and RSET; see line 160). If you do, be sure to use a FIELD statement again before using them for a record.

Lines 30 through 110 display the instructions and the menu, then get the user's request.

Line 130 ends the program. Note the END used to stop the program from moving on to line 140. *Always* CLOSE a file before you END a program or you might lose some or all of the data.

Line 140 sets the variable C to the first available record in the file. The LOF(1) gives the highest used record number. If none have been used it is 0. The LOF(1) + 1 sets C to the next record following the highest record number used – that is, the next record not containing any data.

Line 150 gets a name and phone number.

Line 160 assigns data to be stored in a record. In this case the name (N$) is associated with the FIELDed variable A$ and is stored in the first 25 bytes of the buffer. If the length of N$ is less than 25 bytes, the remaining bytes are filled with spaces. If N$ is no longer than 25 bytes, only the leftmost 25 bytes are associated with A$. In the same manner P$ is associated with B$. This must be done before you store (PUT) a record. Any FIELDed variables not mentioned with LSET are left unchanged in the buffer (assuming a GET was used to move the record into the buffer earlier) and returned to the record when it is stored.

Line 170 stores, in record C of file 1, the data which has just been placed in the file 1 buffer. The 1 after the PUT is the file number.

In line 180 we return to the menu.

Line 190 gets us the name to be searched for.

In line 200 we search the file for a matching name. This will be described starting with line 1000.

In line 210 we return to the menu.

Line 220 begins the routine to change a name and/or phone number. Line 230 gets the name, line 240 searches for it. If the name was not found in the 1000 subroutine, FL is set to 1 and we go back to the menu. In this case FL is not used.

If the name was found, line 260 tells the user what is happening and we go back to line 150 to get the information and store it. Note that we don't see line 140 this time, so whatever C was set to in the subroutine at line 1000 is used as the record number. This is the record where the old name and phone number were stored.

To delete a name and number we get the names to delete with lines 280 and 290. We then search for the name in line 300. If the search in subroutine 1000 was not successful, FL is set to 1 and we return to the menu with line 310. If we found the name, we set N$ to " ", or null, and go to line 160 to store this. Note the old phone number is returned to the record with line 160, but since the associated name is gone, the number will never be retrieved.

In the subroutine at line 400 we get a name, and at 500 the phone number.

The subroutine beginning at line 1000 searches the file for the name in N$ (from line 400). In line 1000 we set both the flag FL and our record number in variable C to 0.

In line 1010 we increment C to point to the next record.

Line 1020 checks to see if the record in C has been used. If C = LOF(1) + 1 is one record beyond the highest numbered record used so far, we go to line 1060, since we must not have found a match to the name in N$ in any of the records used.

In line 1030 we get the contents of record C in variables A$ and B$ (those that were FIELDed). Line 1040 checks to see if the stored name, now in A$, matches the one we are looking for, which is N$. Note that we have to match on the characters in A$ only to LEN(N$) because of the spaces that might have been added to the name in A$ if LEN(A$)<25. (See line 160.) If there is a match we go to line 1070.

If we get to line 1050, there was no match in line 1040, so we go on to the next record via line 1010.

If C is incremented beyond the end of the used records in line 1010, then line 1020 sent us to line 1060 where we tell the user the name was not found, set the flag FL to 1 to notify any calling routine that we didn't find the name, and then branch to line 1090.

If the name was found in line 1040, we print the name and phone number in lines 1070 and 1080. Note that FL is still 0 in this case.

Line 1090 returns us from the subroutine.

This example illustrates the use of random files, but it is pretty wasteful programming. Only 50 bytes of each 128 byte record were used. We'll see some more efficient methods in the next example.

The important things to note are: 1) we only used the FIELD statement once; 2) when we stored a new record we didn't GET it first; 3) the use of LOF in lines 120 and 1040; 4) the FL flag used in the 1000 subroutine; and 5) the comparison method in line 1040. Also note the use of subroutines and GOTOs to eliminate redundant program lines.

If you store a record as record 1, then another as record 200, BASIC creates all the records between them – you have used up the disk space for 200 records, even though you only stored data in two of them. Here's a somewhat more complicated example. In this program we are going to store some inventory records. Each inventory item will have an inventory number (starting at 0 and increasing by ones), description, price, cost, and quantity in stock. The data is organized as follows:

Inventory number – record number
Description   – 20 characters
Price   – 4 bytes, single precision value
Cost   – 4 bytes, single precision value
Quantity   – 2 bytes, integer value

Note that the total storage for a single item is only 30 bytes. A record holds 128 bytes, so we will store four inventory items in each record, leaving only eight bytes per record unused.
We will use the menu from the previous program.

```
10 CLEAR 500 : OPEN "R",1,"INVENTORY"
20 PRINT "MENU"
30 PRINT "1: ADD A NEW ITEM"
40 PRINT "2: RETRIEVE AN ITEM"
50 PRINT "3: CHANGE AN ITEM"
60 PRINT "4: DELETE AN ITEM"
70 PRINT "5: FINISH"
80 INPUT "YOUR CHOICE";A : IF A<1 OR A>5 THEN PRINT
     "BAD CHOICE" : GOTO 80
90 ON A GOTO 110,150,180,240,100
100 CLOSE : END
110 GOSUB 1000
120 GOSUB 1100
130 GOSUB 1200
140 GOTO 20
150 GOSUB 1000
160 GOSUB 1300
170 GOTO 20
180 GOSUB 1000
190 GOSUB 1300
```

```
200 PRINT "NEW DATA?"
210 GOSUB 1100
220 GOSUB 1200
230 GOTO 20
240 GOSUB 1000
250 GOSUB 1300
260 INPUT "OK TO DELETE (Y/N)";AN$ : IF AN$<>"Y"
    THEN 240
270 DE$ = "DELETED"
280 GOSUB 1200
290 GOTO 20

1000 INPUT "INVENTORY NUMBER";IN
1010 RN = INT(IN/4) + 1 : LR = IN
1020 LR = LR - 4 : IF LR>3 THEN 1020
1030 FIELD 1,30*LR AS Z$,20 AS A$,4 AS B$,4 AS C$,2 AS D$
1040 GET 1,RN
1050 RETURN

1100 LINE INPUT "DESCRIPTION? ";DE$ : IF LEN(DE$)>20
     THEN PRINT "TOO LONG" : GOTO 1100
1110 INPUT "PRICE";PR
1120 INPUT "COST";CO
1130 INPUT "QUANTITY";QU%
1140 RETURN

1200 LSET A$ = DE$ : LSET B$ = MKS$(PR) :
     LSET C$ = MKS$(CO) : LSET D$ = MKI$(QU%)
1210 PUT 1,RN
1220 RETURN

1300 IF LEFT$(A$,7) = "DELETED" THEN PRINT "DELETED" :
     GOTO 1330
1310 PRINT "DESCRIPTION";TAB(22);"PRICE";TAB(30);"COST";
     TAB(38);"QUANTITY"
1320 PRINT A$;TAB(22);CVS(B$);TAB(30);CVS(C$);TAB(38);
     CVI(D$)
1330 RETURN
```

I'll skip explaining the obvious lines.

In line 1010 we find the record containing the inventory number. Thus record 1 contains inventory numbers 0, 1, 2, and 3; record 2 contains inventory numbers 4, 5, 6, and 7; etc.

In line 1020 we find out which of the four logical records (our 30 byte records) contains the inventory number we want. LR will end up with 0 if it is the first subrecord, 1 if the second, etc.

Line 1030 FIELDs the entire record into the buffer. The first item after FIELD 1, the 30*LR AS Z$, skips the subrecords in front of the one we want. Thus, if we want, the first subrecord LR will be 0, and 30*0 = 0, so Z$ will not take any space. If we want the third subrecord, 30*2 AS Z$ will skip the first 60 bytes (the first two subrecords) by putting them in Z$, which we never look at.

In line 1040 we GET the record. Note you must always GET the whole record before you store any data in it when using subrecords this way. This keeps any subrecord not mentioned in the FIELD and LSET lines from being changed.

You should be able to figure out the rest of the program.

The LSET cannot be used to reference the same variable. That is, you cannot say LSET A$ = A$ if you don't want to change A$; you must use T$ = A$: LSET A$ = T$ instead. Remember, you cannot use a FIELDed variable to contain data anywhere else in a program without having to re-FIELD it.

LSET means store the data, starting at the left end of the buffer area FIELDed by that variable, adding spaces on the right if the data is too short to fill the buffer area, or chop it (truncate it) on the right if it is too long. You can also use RSET instead of LSET. It means put the last character of the data in the rightmost end of the FIELDed buffer area, adding spaces or truncating the left end of the data. Usually LSET is used. Figure 8-1 illustrates how FIELD, RSET and LSET are used.

The inventory program could use a little improvement. How could you change subroutine 1100 so that when changing data you could just reply with a CR to retain data you didn't want to change without typing it in again? How could you make the program tell you when you try to retrieve an inventory number you haven't used? Hint: see what's stored in an unused record and test for it. If you have a printer, add a selection to the menu that will print out the entire inventory, skipping deleted and unused records. How could you use the MOD operator instead of the one I use in line 1020?

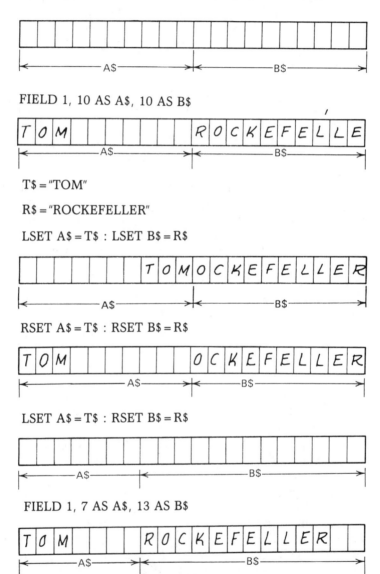

FIELD 1, 10 AS A$, 10 AS B$

T$ = "TOM"

R$ = "ROCKEFELLER"

LSET A$ = T$: LSET B$ = R$

RSET A$ = T$: RSET B$ = R$

LSET A$ = T$: RSET B$ = R$

FIELD 1, 7 AS A$, 13 AS B$

LSET A$ = T$: LSET B$ = R$

Figure 8-1. FIELD, RSET and LSET

Note: in some computers the LOF value is not advanced when you add a record beyond the original LOF value. In this case use CLOSE, OPEN and FIELD after PUTing any record set to a record number beyond the orginal LOF value. This sets the LOF value correctly for the next reference to LOF. You could put this in a subroutine.

Chapter Nine

Additional Useful Features

H ere are some more BASIC commands and statements you will find useful.

AUTO (EXTENDED): This command causes the BASIC interpreter to write the line numbers for you when you are entering a program. Typing AUTO will give you a line number, starting at 10, in increments of 10, each time you enter a CR. To exit AUTO type a control-C. AUTO also permits you to start with any line number and use any increments. For example, if you wish to start with line 100 use

```
AUTO 100
```

This will start with line 100 and use increments of 10 for each new line. If you use

```
AUTO 100,50
```

then the line numbers will start at 100 and advance in increments of 50 (100, 150, 200, 250, etc.). If you should wish to start at 10 with increments of 20, use

```
AUTO 10,20
```

AUTO is used as a command. It cannot be used as a program statement.

If you use AUTO to generate line numbers when editing an existing program, BASIC will print an asterisk after any line number it generates that corresponds to a line that already exists in the program. If you do not wish to change that line use control-C to exit.

CALL (EXTENDED): This statement is used to call a user machine language program. See also the USR command later in this chapter.

```
100 MYPROG=&HD000
110 CALL MYPROG(I,J,K)
120 . . . . . . . . .
```

First you have to put the address of your machine language program in a variable, as in line 100 above. The variable cannot be an array variable. The list of variables (I, J and K) following the address variable are used to pass values from the program to the machine language program. The user-written machine language program is expected to properly deal with the passed values. It is a bit easier to pass values with CALL than with USR. Check your BASIC-80 documentation for a detailed explanation of how to use CALL. (This information was in Appendix C in my manual.) Writing and using machine language programs with BASIC programs is beyond the scope of this book.

CHAIN (DISK): If you wish to have one program load another, this is the command to use. There are several options available.

```
1000 CHAIN "PROG1"
```

loads the program PROG1 into memory, displacing the program that called PROG1. No variables are passed to PROG1. Execution of PROG1 begains at the first line of that program.

```
1000 CHAIN "PROG1",2000
```

is the same as the preceding version, except in this case PROG1 begins at line 2000, even if there are lines preceding this line.

```
1000 CHAIN "PROG1",2000,ALL
```

is the same as the preceding version, except that all variables used in the calling program are available to PROG1. Also see the COMMON statement in this chapter for another way to pass variables to a CHAINed program.

```
1000 CHAIN MERGE"PROG1",2000
```

This version MERGEs PROG1 with the program already in memory. In this case, PROG1 must be an ASCII file, that is, saved on diskette with the A suffix. See Chapter 8, *The Disk*, for more details. Any line numbers in the MERGEd program that duplicate lines in the program already in memory will replace those lines. The 2000 causes the MERGEd program to begin execution at line 2000.

```
1000 CHAIN MERGE"PROG1",2000,DELETE 1000-5000
```

This last version of CHAIN operates as does the last example, with the added option of DELETEing lines 1000 to 5000 in the program being MERGEd to, before the MERGE takes place. This could be used to provide room for the program to be MERGEd or to get rid of conflicting line numbers.

If the original program contained DEFSTR, DEFINT, DEFDBL, DEFSNG, DEFFN statements these variables' types or user defined functions are not passed with the ALL option unless MERGE is also used.

COMMON (DISK): This statement is used to pass specific variables from one program to another. It is usually used with the CHAIN statement. The ALL option used with CHAIN passes all the variables to the CHAINed program. If you only want to pass selected variables you would use COMMON. The COMMON statement consists of the word COMMON followed by a list of the variables to be passed. More than one COMMON statement can appear in a program, but the same variable must not appear in more than one COMMON statement in a program. COMMON statements can appear anywhere in a program, but they are usually placed at the beginning of the program. An example:

```
200 COMMON A$,B,C#,D$( )
300 CHAIN "PROG1",10
```

The variables A$, B, C#, and the array D$( ) are now available to PROG1. Any other variables are lost after line 300. PROG1 will begin with line 10.

DEFINT (EXTENDED): This statement is used to designate a variable or group of variables as integer type, eliminating the need to add a % to the end of each variable. Thus,

```
10 DEFINT A,C,X-Z
```

defines the variable names beginning with A, C, X, Y, and Z as integer variables. Any time a variable beginning with one of these names and no specific overriding type designation is used (ADD$, CHOICE#, etc.), the variable is automatically designated as an integer variable. Since most programs use mostly integer variables (or could do so), and since integer variables take less memory, it might be a good idea to begin every program with DEFINT A-Z and specify any other variables with ! for single precision, # for double precision, and $ for string.

DEFSNG (EXTENDED): This statement is like DEFINT but for single precision variables. Usually this statement is not used since DEFSNG is the default and is assumed by BASIC for all variables unless otherwise specified.

DEFDBL (EXTENDED): This statement is like DEFINT but for double precision variables.

DEFSTR (EXTENDED): This statement is like DEFINT but for string variables.

DEFFN (8K): Here is a useful feature of BASIC. It permits you to write your own functions, like BASIC's SQR, LOG, etc. As mentioned earlier, LOG returns the log of the number to base e. Let's create a function to return the common log (base 10).

```
10 DEF FNCL(X) = LOG(X)*.4343
```

Now if we use

```
50 A = FNCL(20)
```

the common log of 20 will be returned. Another example:

```
10 DEF FNA(X,Y,Z) = (X + Y)*Z
20 A = FNA(10,20,3)
```

A will be set to the sum of 10 and 20 multiplied by 3, or 90. The variables X, Y, and Z in the previous example are called dummy variables. They are only used to demonstrate the desired procedures in the DEF FN statement. These variables can also be used elsewhere in the program without affecting their use in the DEF FN line.

In 8K only one variable can be used in the DEF FN statement. Thus the first example, the common LOG, would be legal in 8K, but the second example using three variables would not be. In EXTENDED you can use more than one variable.

The dummy variables can be replaced by any constant, variable, or expression. Thus:

```
10 DEF FNA(X,Y,Z) = X + Y + Z
20 .........
100 A = FNA(B,C + 9,100)
```

In extended you can also use string variables. Thus,

```
10 DEF FNA$(B$,X) = MID$(B$,X,3)
20 G$ = FNA$("SUNMONTUEWEDTHUFRISAT",C)
```

when asked nicely will return the abbreviation of a day of the week.

Obviously, the DEF FN statement must appear before it is used in a statement.

DEFUSR (EXTENDED): This statement is used to specify the memory address of a machine language subroutine. See USR for examples of accessing these subroutines.

You can define up to 10 of these addresses. The address itself can be an integer constant, expression or variable. Let's define three USR addresses now.

```
10 DEFUSR0 = 23000
20 DEFUSR1 = &HFF00
30 DEFUSR2 = (Y + 1000)
```

The digit after USR can be any single digit (0 through 9). If no digit is used BASIC will consider it USR0.

DELETE (EXTENDED): This command is used to delete one or more program statements. If you wish to delete statements while a program is running, this won't work. BASIC always returns to command level after this statement. If the line number does not exist you will get an error. Here are three ways to use DELETE.

```
DELETE 40
DELETE 40-100
DELETE -40
```

The first example DELETEs one line, number 40. The second DELETEs all the lines from 40 to 100, including lines 40 and 100. The last DELETEs all lines up to and including line 40.

ERR (EXTENDED): This statement is used to test for a specific error. The BASIC error codes are listed in Appendix C. Thus

```
1000 IF ERR=14 THEN ......
```

ERL (EXTENDED): This statement is used to test which line caused an error. Thus

```
1000 IF ERR=15 AND ERL=400 THEN ......
```

ERL and **ERR (8K)**: These statements are used with the ON ERROR... statements described later in this chapter. The ERL variable contains the line number containing the error, ERR contains the code number of the error (see Appendix C).

ERROR (EXTENDED): This statement is also used with the ON ERROR... routines. It is used to simulate an error to test the error trapping routine. Examples are given with ON ERROR... later in this chapter.

This statement also allows you to provide your own error codes. With this release BASIC error messages run to 67. Let's start these new errors at 99 and work down. Here's an example program fragment.

```
990 ON ERROR GOTO 2000
1000 INPUT "MOVE WHICH CHESS PIECE";P$
```

```
1010 INPUT "FROM (X,Y)";A,B
1020 INPUT "TO (X,Y)";C,D
1030 IF C<1 THEN ERROR 99
1040 IF D>8 THEN ERROR 98
1050 IF P$ = "PAWN" and C<D THEN ERROR 97
1060 . . . . . . . .
2000 IF ERR = 99 THEN PRINT "OFF LEFT EDGE OF BOARD" :
     RESUME 1020
2010 IF ERR = 98 THEN PRINT "OFF RIGHT EDGE OF BOARD" :
     RESUME 1020
2020 IF ERR = 97 THEN PRINT "PAWNS MUST MOVE FORWARD"
     : RESUME 1020
2030 ON ERROR GOTO 0
```

The ON ERROR GOTO 0 is used to catch any errors lines
2000 to 2020 missed. It defaults to the normal BASIC error
routine which stops the program and announces the error.
This is obviously not the way to write a chess program.
However, you can see how it is possible to give particular,
though legal, program responses a special error code so they
will be trapped by the program. Sometimes this is easier than
checking every input statement for errors.

An example using most of the error statements follows.

```
10 ON ERROR GOTO 2000
20 INPUT "MONTH";M$
30 INPUT "YEAR";Y
40 IF Y<1000 THEN ERROR = 99
50 INPUT "DAY OF WEEK";D$
60 INPUT "TIME OF DAY";T$
70 IF LEN(T$)<>5 THEN ERROR = 98
80 . . . . . . . .
2000 IF ERR = 13 AND ERL = 20 THEN RESUME 3000
2010 IF ERR = 99 THEN PRINT "USE FOUR DIGITS" : RESUME 30
2020 IF ERR = 13 AND ERL = 50 THEN PRINT "USE DAY, NOT
     DATE" : RESUME
2030 IF ERR = 98 THEN PRINT "USE 00:00 PATTERN" :
     RESUME 0
2040 ON ERROR GOTO 0
3000 PRINT "USE NAME OF MONTH, NOT NUMBER" : GOTO 20
```

So you can see there are many possibilities for creative error
trapping. Use your imagination; I only listed a few possible
techniques.

FRE (8K): This function is used to find out how much memory, or string space, is still available to the program. It can be used within a program or as a command. If the variable following FRE is a numeric variable, FRE(X) for example, the number of bytes of memory not being used by the program are returned. If a string variable is used, for example FRE(X$), or FRE(" "), the number of bytes of string space not being used by the program will be returned.

Because Microsoft BASIC permits you to store strings of any length in string variables without declaring each variable's length beforehand, you must put up with what is called *garbage collecting*. When you use FRE(X$) or run out of string space, BASIC must go through the string area and remove any old strings that are no longer used. This takes time: anywhere from a few seconds to over a minute. So when you use FRE(X$) you can expect a delay of some length. Note that the X and X$ used in the examples are dummy variables. Any valid variable name can be used, and it will have no effect on any data stored in that variable.

INP (8K): This function is used to allow BASIC to get data from the outside world. Assuming that you have the hardware to support the statement in your computer, A = INP(X) reads the parallel data port X and stores the byte read in variable A. To work properly, the device supplying the data should respond only to the address X in the statement. This will eliminate the possibility of several devices supplying data to the same INP statement. Also check to be sure you are not conflicting with any data ports used by the computer (disk drives, cassette ports, etc.).

INPUT$ (DISK): This statement can be used two ways. If you use A$ = INPUT$(X,#Y), then A$ will contain X number of bytes of data read from disk file #Y. It is assumed that this file has been properly OPENed previously (See chapter 8 for disk operation.)

If you use A$ = INPUT$(X), then the program expects X number of bytes to be provided by the keyboard. The keyboard data is not echoed on the CRT or printer. This could be used, for example, if you wanted to get a password from the operator but did not wish the password to echo on the screen for security. All control characters except control-C are passed through. Control-C will stop execution of INPUT$.

LLIST (EXTENDED): This command is used like the LIST command except that it prints the listing on the line printer. All variations of LIST are included. The LLIST command is not included in all implementations of BASIC-80.

LPOS (8K): This function is the same as the POS function, but it is used to find the print head position of the line printer. See POS for details.

ON ERROR GOTO (EXTENDED): This statement is used to trap program errors. If you wish to eliminate, or at least decrease, the number of program crashes (unplanned program terminations), you should use this statement. It tells the program where to find instructions on what to do in case of a program error. For example, if you have the statement

```
205 B = C/D
```

and you had just INPUT D, and D was made equal to zero, you would get an error message (you can't divide by 0) and the program would stop and go into command mode. This, of course, would ruin the program run. If, however, you had an ON ERROR GOTO statement in the program and the divide by zero error occurred, the program could branch to a program error message (not BASIC error message), tell the operator a zero was invalid input, and return to the offending statement for another try.

OUT (8K): This statement works like INP but it is used to output a byte from a computer parallel port to the outside world. As with INP, your computer must have the proper hardware to implement this statement.

```
OUT P,B
```

where P is the port number and B the byte of data to be output. Usually your external hardware is designed to respond to the data byte only upon receiving the correct port number.

POS (8K): This function returns the current cursor position. Thus using

```
10 A = POS(X) : IF A<40 THEN . . .
```

would get the cursor position in the variable A. The X is a

dummy variable and has no effect on the function. You can use any variable here.

RENUM (EXTENDED): This command is used to renumber program lines. If you have run out of room between line numbers or wish to have your varied line number increments all set to one value, then use RENUM. Just entering

```
RENUM
```

as a direct command will renumber all the program lines to a series beginning with 10, and with increments of 10 between each line number. All line number references, for example in GOSUB or GOTO statements, will be adjusted to reflect the new line numbers. You may use any of the following options after RENUM.

```
RENUM (NEW NUMBER),(OLD NUMBER),(INCREMENT)
```

NEW NUMBER is the desired first program line number. The default is 10 if it is not entered.

OLD NUMBER is the program line number where you wish to start the new line numbers. Note that by using this option you can renumber only parts of the program, or start subroutines with distinctive higher line numbers. If this option is not used, the default is the first program line number.

INCREMENT is the number of line numbers to skip between line numbers used.

```
RENUM 100,10,100
```

would start the line numbers at 100, beginning with your original line number 10, increments of 100. If you used

```
RENUM 10,,20
```

the renumbering would start the line numbers at 10, beginning with your first program line, in increments of 20. Note how you retain the commas if you leave out one of the three optional values.

RESUME (EXTENDED): This statement is used to tell BASIC what to do after an error is trapped.

RESUME	Causes program to RESUME execution at the line causing the error.
RESUME 0	Same as RESUME.
RESUME NEXT	Program execution RESUMEs at the line following the line containing the error.
RESUME 1000	Program resumes execution at any line number (1000 in the example).

TRON/TROFF (EXTENDED): These statements are used to trace program progress. TRON turns on the trace, TROFF turns it off. TRON can be used as a direct command or in a program. Every line number reached by BASIC after it sees the TRON statement is displayed between a pair of brackets across and then down the screen. This can be useful to see just where a program crashes or whether it follows the program logic as you had planned. Program lines will continue to be printed, even after the program is restarted, unless you use TROFF as a command to turn off the trace.

USR (8K): This function is used when you wish to run a machine language segment from inside your program. A machine language RETURN at the end of the machine language segment gets you back to BASIC. In 8K BASIC you can only define one USR statement at a time.

```
DEFUSR = &H7018 : A = USR(X)
```

Of course the two statements do not have to be on the same line. In EXTENDED BASIC you can have up to 10 USR statements active. Thus

```
DEFUSR9 = &H7018 : A = USR9(X)
```

where you can substitute any single digit from 0 through 9 for the 9 in the example. This permits setting up 10 different USR calls. The X in parentheses following USR is any numeric or string expression. This X is then passed to the machine language program segment. If you have more than one value to pass, you can POKE the values into protected memory for the machine language program to retrieve. After returning to BASIC, any values passed back by the machine language program can be found by using PEEK to predetermined addresses; one value can also be returned in the variable used in the USR statement, X in this case.

Using USR is rather complex and the advanced user who wishes to learn more should consult the BASIC documentation (Appendix C in my manual). See also DEFUSR in this chapter for details on how to set the USR call's address in EX-TENDED BASIC. In 8K you must use POKE to store the address of the USR segment in a specific pair of bytes in memory. This location varies, depending on the computer used. See your documentation for details.

VARPTR (EXTENDED): This function is used to find the address where a string variable is stored, together with its length, or it points to the location where a numeric variable is stored. It is usually used with USR to pass the value of a variable to a machine language subroutine. Using

    X = VARPTR(A)

puts the address of the first byte of data identified with variable A in variable X. The variable can be any type: string, numeric, or array. If the value returned in X is negative, add 65536 to it to obtain the actual address. Note that array variable locations are changed every time a new non-array variable is used. So use VARPTR immediately before the USR call – and don't use a new variable in the USR call!

VARPTR# (DISK): This function is like VARPTR but it is used to find the address of file buffers for use in a machine language subroutine. Thus,

    X = VARPTR # (A)

will put the address of the disk I/O buffer assigned to the file number A. If A is the number of a random file, the address is that of the FIELDed buffer.

WAIT (8K): This statement is used like INP but it WAITs for a specific input byte before the program continues.

    WAIT A,I,J

will look at port A (default 0), and XOR any byte received with J (default 0), and AND the result with I. You must supply

I; A and J are optional. If the result of the XOR and AND is not 0, then the WAIT is resumed. If the result is 0, the program continues.

WIDTH (EXTENDED): This statement (or command) is used to set the width (length) of the lines displayed.

WIDTH 64

would set the displayed line length to 64 characters. At that point BASIC inserts a carriage return (CHR$(13)) to start a new line. The value after WIDTH can be any expression that resolves to an integer value between 15 and 255. The default (if WIDTH is not used) is 72. If the value used is 255, the line is considered to be of infinite length and no carriage return is ever inserted.

You can use the same command to set the line length on your line printer. In this case

WIDTH (LPRINT) 132

sets the line printer line length at 132 characters.

Chapter Ten

The BASIC Compiler

This is not going to be a detailed chapter on how to use a compiler, but an explanation of how one works and what it can do for you.

The compiler in question is the Microsoft BASIC Compiler, and it is designed to work with Microsoft BASIC. It is available for most computers and operating systems. It is disk based; that is, it requires at least one disk drive to use it. The compiler is not part of Microsoft BASIC; it must be purchased separately.

When you are running a program in BASIC, BASIC acts as an *interpreter*. Every line of the BASIC program is converted to machine language and acted upon each time the interpreter sees it. If you have a loop, for example

```
10 FOR X = 1 TO 1000
20 PRINT X*3.14159
30 NEXT X
```

the interpreter must convert line 20 to machine language and perform the computation 1000 times. The number 3.14159 must be converted to binary floating point each time, and the multiplication routines must be called and used each time.

When a program is compiled, the lines are converted to machine language. These machine language instructions are used to create a new program (in machine language). The original program is called the *source program*, the machine language version the *object program* (or object file). So now the conversion of each line only occurs once, when the program is compiled. The advantage is that the program now runs faster, 10 to 40 times faster depending on program content.

If your programs are the type that spend most of their time waiting for a user's response or displaying data, then the compiler doesn't have much advantage. However, if a lot of program time is spent in loops, calculations, and string manipulation, then the compiler can be a great asset.

Normally a compiler has a big disadvantage – debugging. You write a program, compile it, then run it. If there is an error, you can't just use BASIC's command mode to tell you what is in the applicable variables, rewrite what appears to be the offending line, and try another run. First you must get the original (source) program back into memory, edit it, then save it back onto the disk. Next you must recompile the edited program. Compiling takes time, at least a few minutes, longer for a lengthy program. Also, you can't get the variable values like you can with BASIC's command mode. You usually must add PRINT statements to the program to keep track of the variable's values. Some compilers have a way to check variable contents, but it usually is not so convenient as using BASIC's command mode. In any event, you still have to edit the source program and recompile. So you can see that using a compiler can be a slow process until you get the program completely debugged because of the need to recompile after every program bug shows up and an attempt is made to correct it. Also, it is frequently difficult to determine the actual statement causing the error if the compiler error system doesn't use your source code line numbers.

Using the BASIC interpreter to run a program and debug it, then compiling it for speed gives you the best of both worlds. However, most compilers don't include an interpreter.

Almost all of the Microsoft BASIC interpreter statements can be used in a program to be compiled with the Microsoft BASIC Compiler (hereafter to be called BASIC and BASCOM). The exceptions are the cassette commands, CLEAR, DELETE, LOAD, SAVE, and others of this nature. The CLEAR statement is not needed, and the others are not generally used within a program. You can use CHAIN and LOAD to RUN another program module and use USR to call machine language routines.

There are two BASIC statements that you might wish were present in BASCOM. ERASE is not allowed. You can DIM an array but you must use constants for the array size, not a variable or expression. Thus DIM A(20) is OK but DIM A(X) or DIM A(3 + 5) is not. You must be a little more careful about numeric expressions. For example

```
10 I% = 20000
20 J% = -18000
30K% = 20000
40 M% = I% + J% + K%
```

In BASIC there would be no problem. But BASCOM might perform line 40 as M% = I% + K% + J% instead of the order set in line 40. This would give I% + K%, or 40000, which is beyond the integer range of M%. So you must be careful to use parentheses to be sure BASCOM does the calculations in the order you desire.

```
40 M% = (I% + J%) + K%
```

Not a big problem, but you must be aware of the possibilities and plan ahead.

With the above exceptions you can take almost any program that will run under BASIC and run it under BASCOM with no problems. I've been using BASCOM for several years with complete success.

A disadvantage of BASCOM is the size of the compiled program. It is usually larger than the BASIC source program, sometimes a great deal larger. In addition, a runtime program called BRUN must be included in memory with the object file. However, if you have ample memory and need the speed, BASCOM is the way to go.

I had one business program that required about an hour to make an involved calculation requiring many large loops and many string manipulations. The compiled version runs it in less than two minutes. I can't promise such a dramatic difference in all programs, but the difference will be appreciable. One trick to using BASCOM, and BASIC as well, is to use integer variables wherever possible, especially in FOR loops, and use variables instead of constants wherever possible.

BASCOM OPERATION

First thoroughly debug your program by running it with the interpreter. Make sure there are no ERASE, COMMON, or DIMs using variables or expressions. Now delete any CLEAR statements. Next SAVE the program in ASCII by adding the ,A suffix. You might need to add a special filename extension such as .BAS in CP/M.

Next compile the program. We won't give the actual commands because they vary with the DOS used. Also, they are given in detail in the BASCOM manual. You can get a listing file and/or a relative file, or no file if you are just testing for errors. The listing file is not necessary; it is a long file which lists the compiled code in assembly language. The relative file is necessary to get the final object file. This takes only a minute or two.

Next you use the LINK-80 loader (linking loader) to link the relative file with the library routines to create the object program. This will take another minute or two. Next SAVE the linked object file to disk.

Now you have a completed compiled program. To use it on some systems you must have the BRUN module, supplied with the compiler. BRUN loads your object file and supplies some of the common routines required to run the object file.

There are a number of switches you can add to the compile and link commands. An example is adding /E to tell BASCOM you have some ON ERROR GOTO statements in the program. There are several other switches for special conditions the compiler needs to know about. Don't be too concerned: either you usually won't use any switches, or you'll almost always use one or two of them—it all depends on your program style and types of programs you usually write.

If BASCOM sounds like something you need, you should check on it. It is easy to use and will really speed up your BASIC programs. The best part is you can debug your program with the interpreter before you compile it. This is a big advantage over most compilers which only compile some of the BASIC lines, or which will not work with Microsoft BASIC and don't offer an interpreter for their version of BASIC.

This was just a very brief overview of the Microsoft Compiler. All the details of its operation are outlined in the manual included with the compiler.

Chapter Eleven

Radio Shack BASIC

You Radio Shack computer owners may have noticed a great deal of similarity between your TRS-80 BASIC and the BASIC described in this book.

Well, both versions were written by the same people, Microsoft, and most of the instructions and defaults are the same.

Here are the exceptions noted in using the BASIC provided with the TRS-80 Model III computer, and the TRSDOS 1.3 disk operating system provided for the Model III. TRSDOS was not written by Microsoft, but does contain similar instructions. Only those DOS instructions duplicated in Microsoft BASIC are included in this summary. TRSDOS contains many additional commands as well.

Here are the commands mentioned for Microsoft BASIC that don't exist in Model III BASIC. Note, except for the following deletions and changes, the TRS-80 BASIC is the same as Microsoft EXTENDED BASIC.

These commands don't exist in Model III BASIC.

```
ERASE
OPTION BASE
NULL
LINE INPUT (in DISK version)
SWAP
HEX$( )
OCT$( )
&H (in DISK version)
&0 (in DISK version)
```

XOR (logic)
EQV (logic)
IMP (logic)
\ (integer division)
MOD (modulus)
DEFFN (in DISK version)
INSTR (in DISK version)
No single $ in PRINT USING
No control-A in editing
No beep for invalid input when editing
CONSOLE
CONTROL-O
CONTROL-G
WAIT
RENUM (in DISK version)
WIDTH (only for line printer with FORMS command)

That's a long list, but you'll note that most are seldom-used commands. If needed, there is generally a way to program around them. In my experience I find they are a very small loss in most of my programming.

The following are changes from Microsoft BASIC to Model III BASIC that accomplish the same end result.

MICROSOFT	TRS-80
CR	ENTER
LF	DOWN ARROW
@	SHIFT LEFT ARROW
, (14 column)	, (15 column)
DELETE	LEFT ARROW
RUBOUT	LEFT ARROW
CONTROL-C	BREAK
CONTROL-S	SHIFT @ (use any key to restart)
FRE(0)	MEM
SPACE$( )	USE STRING$(X," ")

In editing, use SHIFT UP ARROW to ESCAPE.
In PRINT USING, use % instead of \ for strings.
Instead of ERR, use ERR/2 + 1 in error trapping routines.
The USR statement is held to a single call in MODEL III BASIC, 11 calls in DISK BASIC.

You can't RESTORE to a specific line number in Model III BASIC. That wasn't so bad, was it? Most of the statements are the same so it is very easy to use the information you learned in this book with few changes. The DISK BASICs are just about identical. The only differences are that TRSDOS (MODEL III DISK BASIC and operating system) doesn't include the OCT$( ) and HEX$( ) statements. TRSDOS does include several disk utilities that are not provided in Microsoft DISK BASIC. However, the DOS that is used with Microsoft DISK BASIC generally provides these or similar added utilities.

Here are a few examples. DIR is used to get a list of files and their attributes that are contained on a diskette. BACKUP is used to copy an entire diskette. COPY is used to copy single files. FORMAT is used to prepare a new or erased diskette for use. You can password protect access to programs and data files. You have a built-in, not very accurate clock that can be accessed by your programs. FREE tells you how much space you have left on a diskette. LIST displays or prints the contents of a file. SETCOM is used to set up the specifications for a serial printer or a modem. There are others as well.

The DISK BASIC supplied with TRSDOS will do just about everything Microsoft DISK BASIC does, plus a few more goodies. You can disable the BREAK (control-C) key during a program run. You can print or display a list of all the variables in a program (or selected ones) and their associated line numbers. You can use MID$( ) to the left of the equals sign.

Now for the good news. The TRS-80 allows you to do some things that are not possible with Microsoft BASIC (BASIC-80 Ver. 5.0). Remember, Microsoft wrote the Model III BASIC too! There are four very powerful graphics commands: SET( ), RESET( ), POINT( ), and PRINT@.

The SET( ) statement permits you to light a small area on the display; the RESET( ) statement permits you to turn off a lighted area; the POINT( ) statement lets you check to see if an area is on or off; and the PRINT@ statement lets you print in any area of the display without affecting the rest of the display.

In using SET, RESET, and POINT, the CRT screen is divided in 6144 segments, 128 segments across, 48 down. Thus you can draw graphs, charts, or pictures using this, for example, a football field or outlines of cards for a cardgame. You have the CRT screen for your canvas and you are the artist.

The SET(X,Y) statement turns on the screen segment to position X (0 to 127) across the screen and position Y (0 to 47) down the screen. The Radio Shack manual provides a diagram showing the number and location of each screen segment.

The RESET(X,Y) statement turns off the screen segment specified by X and Y. If it is not turned on, RESET has no effect.

The POINT(X,Y) statement returns a −1 if the indicated screen segment is turned on, 0 if not.

The PRINT@ statement permits starting a display line at any character position on the screen (64 across, 16 down).

With a little imagination you can do a lot of things with these commands.

You can also use string commands to print graphics. Each character position can contain a graphic block, which can be any of 64 different shapes (see TRS-80 manual). You can print these graphic blocks with STRING$( ), PRINT, PRINT@, and other string functions. The graphic blocks are printed with the CHR$( ) function, the argument being the graphic block code (128–191).

The TRS-80 Model III can also display many other special characters not shown in the ASCII list, such as Greek characters, mathematical symbols, Japanese Kana characters, other foreign letters, and many other characters. All are listed in the TRS-80 Model III manual.

You can direct program output to the display and printer at the same time.

You can "protect" several displayed lines at the top of the screen so they will not be scrolled over as new lines appear after the screen is full.

Chapter Twelve

In Conclusion

I've tried to pass along a lot of the information I've learned the hard way, working with various versions of Microsoft BASIC, from MITS 3.0 to Radio Shack Model III. The BASIC in this book (Microsoft BASIC-80, Ver. 5.0) is the most general version and the most up to date as this is being written.

Most of the data I've given you is in the BASIC documentation, but I've tried to make it a little clearer and add some examples to help you understand it a little better.

I have also tried to spell out alternate forms of the various commands so you can see some of the programming possibilities. I've also given you some short programs to make my point and tried to give you some interesting ideas of ways to modify my programs or write new ones. I hope you have given my suggested programs a try, because there's no better way to learn to program than to write your own program and run it.

Remember, when writing a program define the problem in detail. What should happen if this occurs? Once you have a good grasp of the problem and exactly what you want the program to do in every circumstance, then write it.

Read as much as you can about *top down* and structured programming techniques. If you follow these precepts you will end up with fewer bugs and easier-to-modify programs. It's really a good way to program. Even if you don't write a good structured program the first few times, try to do better on the next ones. You'll soon accept and appreciate the principle.

Be sure to comment your programs liberally. You'll be surprised at how soon you can forget how a tricky little subroutine works. If you can't remember how a program works, you can't readily fix it or add to it.

Don't be afraid to scrap a program and start over again if you have to. You have learned a lot about the program the first time through and the final program will be the better for it.

Don't always proceed with the "brute force" method of programming, coding the first method you think of. Sometimes a little thought will deliver a much simpler, more elegant method of doing the same thing. If you have a disk, use it — for program instructions, files, lists, tables, etc.

Have fun programming. If you're anything like me, you'll find it to be a fantastic hobby and you'll spend a lot of time thinking about programs and computers.

Appendix A

Values of ASCII Characters and Control Keys

DECIMAL	OCTAL	HEX	ASCII CHARACTER OR CONTROL	
Ø	Ø	Ø	CONTROL SHIFT P, NULL	
1	1	1	CONTROL A	
2	2	2	CONTROL B	
3	3	3	CONTROL C	
4	4	4	CONTROL D	
5	5	5	CONTROL E	
6	6	6	CONTROL F	
7	7	7	CONTROL G,	RINGS BELL
8	1Ø	8	CONTROL H,	BACKSPACE ON SOME TERMINALS
9	11	9	CONTROL I	HORIZONTAL TAB ON SOME TERMINALS
1Ø	12	A	CONTROL J,	LINE FEED
11	13	B	CONTROL K	
12	14	C	CONTROL L,	FORM FEED ON SOME TERMINALS
13	15	D	CONTROL M,	CARRIAGE RETURN
14	16	E	CONTROL N	
15	17	F	CONTROL O	
16	2Ø	1Ø	CONTROL P	
17	21	11	CONTROL Q	
18	22	12	CONTROL R	
19	23	13	CONTROL S	
2Ø	24	14	CONTROL T	
21	25	15	CONTROL U	
22	26	16	CONTROL V	
23	27	17	CONTROL W	

DECIMAL	OCTAL	HEX	ASCII CHARACTER OR CONTROL
24	3∅	18	CONTROL X
25	31	19	CONTROL Y
26	32	1A	CONTROL Z
27	33	1B	CONTROL SHIFT K, ESCAPE
28	34	1C	CONTROL SHIFT L
29	35	1D	CONTROL SHIFT M
3∅	36	1E	CONTROL SHIFT N
31	37	1F	CONTROL SHIFT O
32	4∅	2∅	SPACE
33	41	21	!
34	42	22	"
35	43	23	#
36	44	24	$
37	45	25	%
38	46	26	&
39	47	27	'
4∅	5∅	28	(
41	51	29	)
42	52	2A	*
43	53	2B	+
44	54	2C	,
45	55	2D	—
46	56	2E	.
47	57	2F	/
48	6∅	3∅	∅
49	61	31	1
5∅	62	32	2
51	63	33	3
52	64	34	4
53	65	35	5
54	66	36	6
55	67	37	7
56	7∅	38	8
57	71	39	9
58	72	3A	:
59	73	3B	;
6∅	74	3C	<
61	75	3D	=
62	76	3E	>
63	77	3F	?
64	1∅∅	4∅	@
65	1∅1	41	A

DECIMAL	OCTAL	HEX	ASCII CHARACTER OR CONTROL
66	1Ø2	42	B
67	1Ø3	43	C
68	1Ø4	44	D
69	1Ø5	45	E
7Ø	1Ø6	46	F
71	1Ø7	47	G
72	11Ø	48	H
73	111	49	I
74	112	4A	J
75	113	4B	K
76	114	4C	L
77	115	4D	M
78	116	4E	N
79	117	4F	O
8Ø	12Ø	5Ø	P
81	121	51	Q
82	122	52	R
83	123	53	S
84	124	54	T
85	125	55	U
86	126	56	V
87	127	57	W
88	13Ø	58	X
89	131	59	Y
9Ø	132	5A	Z
91	133	5B	[
92	134	5C	\
93	135	5D	]
94	136	5E	^
95	137	5F	—
96	14Ø	6Ø	`
97	141	61	a
98	142	62	b
99	143	63	c
1ØØ	144	64	d
1Ø1	145	65	e
1Ø2	146	66	f
1Ø3	147	67	g
1Ø4	15Ø	68	h
1Ø5	151	69	i
1Ø6	152	6A	j
1Ø7	153	6B	k

DECIMAL	OCTAL	HEX	ASCII CHARACTER OR CONTROL
1Ø8	154	6C	l
1Ø9	155	6D	m
11Ø	156	6E	n
111	157	6F	o
112	16Ø	7Ø	p
113	161	71	q
114	162	72	r
115	163	73	s
116	164	74	t
117	165	75	u
118	166	76	v
119	167	77	w
12Ø	17Ø	78	x
121	171	79	y
122	172	7A	z
123	173	7B	{
124	174	7C	|
125	175	7D	}
127	177	7F	DELETE

Appendix B

Reserved Words

Reserved words	Lowest BASIC level which supports function shown
$	8K
%	EXTENDED
!	EXTENDED
#	EXTENDED
&	EXTENDED
'	EXTENDED
ABS	8K
AND	8K
ASC	8K
ATN	8K
AUTO	EXTENDED
CALL	EXTENDED
CDBL	EXTENDED
CHAIN	DISK
CHR$	8K
CINT	EXTENDED
CLEAR	8K
CLOAD	8K
CLOSE	DISK
COMMON	DISK
CONSOLE	EXTENDED
CONT	8K
COS	8K

Reserved words	Lowest BASIC level which supports function shown
CSAVE	8K
CSNG	EXTENDED
CVD	DISK
CVI	DISK
CVS	DISK
DATA	8K
DEF	8K
DEF DBL	EXTENDED
DEF INT	EXTENDED
DEF SNG	EXTENDED
DEF STR	EXTENDED
DEF USR	EXTENDED
DIM	8K
EDIT	EXTENDED
END	8K
EOF	DISK
EQV	8K
ERASE	EXTENDED
ERL	EXTENDED
ERR	EXTENDED
EXP	8K
FIELD	DISK
FILES	DISK
FIX	EXTENDED
FOR	8K
FRE	8K
GET	DISK
GOSUB	8K
GOTO	8K
HEX$	EXTENDED
IF-GOTO	8K
IF-THEN	8K
IF-THEN-ELSE	EXTENDED

Reserved words	Lowest BASIC level which supports function shown
IMP	8K
INKEY$	EXTENDED
INP	8K
INPUT	8K
INPUT#	DISK
INPUT$	DISK
INSTR	EXTENDED
INT	8K
KILL	DISK
LEFT$	8K
LEN	8K
LET	8K
LINE INPUT	EXTENDED
LINE INPUT#	DISK
LIST	8K
LLIST	EXTENDED
LOAD	DISK
LOC	DISK
LOF	DISK
LOG	8K
LPOS	EXTENDED
LPRINT	EXTENDED
LPRINT USING	EXTENDED
LSET	DISK
MERGE	DISK
MID$	8K
MKD$	DISK
MKI$	DISK
MKS$	DISK
MOD	EXTENDED
NAME	DISK
NEW	8K
NEXT	8K
NOT	8K
NULL	8K

Reserved words	Lowest BASIC level which supports function shown
OCT$	EXTENDED
ON ERROR GOTO	EXTENDED
ON-GOSUB	8K
ON-GOTO	8K
OPEN	DISK
OPTION BASE	8K
OR	8K
OUT	8K
PEEK	8K
POKE	8K
POS	8K
PRINT	8K
PRINT USING	EXTENDED
PRINT#	DISK
PRINT# USING	DISK
PUT	DISK
RANDOMIZE	EXTENDED
READ	8K
REM	8K
RENUM	EXTENDED
RESTORE	8K
RESUME	EXTENDED
RESUME NEXT	EXTENDED
RETURN	8K
RND	8K
RIGHT$	8K
RSET	DISK
RUN	8K
SAVE	DISK
SGN	8K
SIN	8K
SPACE$	EXTENDED
SPC	8K
SQR	8K
STOP	8K

Reserved words	Lowest BASIC level which supports function shown
STR$	8K
STRING$	EXTENDED
SWAP	EXTENDED
TAB	8K
TAN	8K
TROFF	EXTENDED
TRON	EXTENDED
USR	8K
VAL	8K
VARPTR	EXTENDED
WAIT	8K
WEND	EXTENDED
WHILE	EXTENDED
WIDTH	EXTENDED
WRITE	DISK
WRITE#	DISK
XOR	8K

Appendix C

Error Messages

CODE	NUMBER	LONG FORM
NF	1	NEXT without FOR
SN	2	Syntax error
RG	3	RETURN without GOSUB
OD	4	Out of data
FC	5	Illegal function call
OV	6	Overflow
OM	7	Out of memory
UL	8	Undefined line
BS	9	Subscript out of range
DD	10	Redimensioned array
/0	11	Division by zero
ID	12	Illegal direct
TM	13	Type mismatch
OS	14	Out of string space
LS	15	String too long
ST	16	String formula too complex
CN	17	Can't continue
UF	18	Undefined user function

Index

MORE HELPFUL WORDS FOR YOU

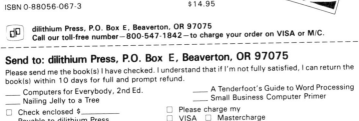